Meet and Write

book one

Meet and Write

A teaching anthology of contemporary poetry
in three books

book one
book two
book three

Meet and Write

*A teaching anthology of
contemporary poetry*

book one

Edited by Sandy and Alan Brownjohn

HODDER AND STOUGHTON

LONDON SYDNEY AUCKLAND TORONTO

British Library Cataloguing in Publication Data
    Meet and write.
    Bk. 1.
    1. English poetry——20th century
    I. Brownjohn, Sandy   II. Brownjohn, Alan
    821'.914'08   PR1174
    ISBN 0 340 37149 8

First published 1985
Third impression 1991
Selection and commentary copyright © 1985 Sandy and Alan Brownjohn

Printed and bound in Great Britain for
Hodder and Stoughton Educational,
a division of Hodder and Stoughton Ltd,
Mill Road, Dunton Green, Sevenoaks, Kent,
by Page Bros (Norwich) Ltd.

Contents

How to Get the Most Out of This Book

Meet and Write is intended to introduce you to the work of modern poets, and at the same time to encourage you to explore the techniques and the craft of poetry by writing for yourself.

There are thirteen poets represented in Book One and each poet has written a personal introduction to the section containing his/her work. At the end of each section there is a brief discussion of the poems, and explanations of the techniques used. There are plenty of suggestions to encourage your own writing, as we believe that trying to write oneself leads to a better understanding of poetry and a greater facility in the use of language.

Every poem has therefore been chosen to illustrate a particular use of language and technique, and we hope this will ensure that there is something for everyone. Above all, we trust that reading these poems and writing your own will be both thought-provoking and enjoyable.

Sandy and Alan Brownjohn

Colin West

I was born during the Festival of Britain in 1951, on the cusp of Taurus and Gemini, and have spent much time thereafter in a similar state of indecision. Unable to decide between a vocation in writing or drawing, I chose to indulge in both.

My childhood was spent in semi-rural Essex — a mixture of pig-sties, country fêtes and Lonnie Donegan. My interests at this stage included Natural History, Conjuring, Poetry and Riding my Bicycle.

I was an undistinguished sportsman. The rules of cricket, rugby and soccer remain a complete mystery to me.

Leaving school at the earliest opportunity to study art, I maintained my interest in words, filling an ever-growing collection of Woolworth notebooks.

The actual writing process is difficult to explain, or even remember. It can take the form of idly playing around with words whilst waiting for a bus, or a more frenzied activity when my pen can hardly capture my thoughts fast enough. But if they *do* escape, perhaps I'll catch them another day.

I think — being interested in visual things — I sometimes have in my head an image (which eventually becomes the accompanying drawing) that helps the poem to come. The line 'Down in the darkest and dingiest dungeon' came to me once, and I began to think of the Cruikshank illustration of Fagin in his condemned cell from *Oliver Twist*. I went to bed with the first line and picture in my head, and throughout a restless night, the poem 'wrote itself'.

Poems don't always come in one rush, though, and after having written the first stanza of 'A Scarecrow Remembers' I came to a dead end. Some weeks later, I thought rather than pursue the scarecrow's thoughts about himself, it would be more interesting if he were to consider his less fortunate 'brother', a November guy. I wrote the rest of the poem quite quickly, not worrying too much about the usual restrictions of regular metre or rhyme that I often impose on myself.

I never sit down and deliberately write a poem. But there are things we can do to coax them out — if we keep our ears and eyes open, keeping a note of all that is funny, sad, odd, entertaining or charming. Let these observations and feelings emerge in their own good time as poems.

The Darkest and Dingiest Dungeon

Down in the darkest and dingiest dungeon,
Far from the tiniest twinkle of stars,
Far from the whiff of a wonderful luncheon,
Far from the murmur of motoring cars,
Far from the habits of rabbits and weasels,
Far from the merits of ferrets and stoats,
Far from the danger of mumps or of measles,
Far from the fashions of fabulous coats,
Far from the turn of a screw in a socket,
Far from the fresh frozen food in the fridge,
Far from the fluff in my dufflecoat pocket,
Far from the bite of a mischievous midge,
Far from the hole in my humble umbrella,
Far from my hat as it hangs in the hall,
I sit here alone with myself in the cellar,
I *do* so like getting away from it all!

A Scarecrow Remembers

Head of straw and heart of wood,
With arms outstretched like this I've stood
For half a year in Hertfordshire,
My feet stuck in the mud.

Things could be worse, for I remember
One day early in November
The children came from far and wide
Wheeling a barrow with another
Ragged fellow flopped inside.
But no sooner had I glimpsed my brother
Than they took him from his carriage
To a hilltop where they perched him on a pyre
And they laughed to watch him perish
As they set his rags on fire.

The sky that night was filled with light,
With shooting stars and rockets.
I stood my ground and made no sound
When sparks fell in my pockets.

Amidst the Bedlam I could see
Old Owl a-tremble in his tree
And when the noise at last died down
The children all returned to town
And left the bonfire smouldering
And my poor brother mouldering
Till only ash remained.

The Darkest and Dingiest Dungeon

This is written to a pattern determined by the first two words of each line — 'Far from'. The place is set — the dungeon — and each line states what it is the poet is 'far from'. Notice the technique of alliteration: many phrases here contain a number of words beginning with the same letter. The title is alliterative: The *D*arkest and *D*ingiest *D*ungeon. (Tongue twisters are frequently based on alliteration, but none of Colin West's lines is difficult to speak.)

Practise writing some alliterative sentences, or even a whole alliterative poem. You could start with the line 'Sat at the *t*op of the *t*allest *t*ree' and make each line that follows begin with 'Watching . . .' When you write other poems later, try to use the occasional alliterative phrase to add colour (and sound effects) to your writing.

A Scarecrow Remembers

Colin West's scarecrow poem takes a new angle on the subject of Guy Fawkes Night. A connection has been made between two man-made figures: the scarecrow and the guy. There has always been a feeling that such figures are almost human, and might have minds and feelings of their own, something which might also be said of ventriloquists' dummies and dolls. You might find it interesting to imagine yourself as one of these figures and write a poem about life as seen through his or her eyes. There are other man-made figures you can write about, for example those used to test the efficiency of car seat-belts, or large cardboard figures which beckon you into supermarkets or cafés. Not to mention the statue you pass in a city street or square and hardly ever notice.

Charles Causley

I was born in 1917 in Launceston, a small Cornish market town on the River Tamar which divides Cornwall from Devon, and where I still live. I was always an avid reader, and the most wonderful ability in the world seemed to me that of being able to write a book; any kind of book. I longed to meet a real live writer, but imagined they all lived in London, which as far as I was concerned in those days might have been on the other side of the moon.

In the meantime, I tried to write books myself: three-page novels, two-page plays, the shortest short stories in literary history, and — above all — poems. I was attracted to writing poems because I thought that they didn't involve as much labour in their production as other literary forms. Time has taught me just how wrong I was in this particular belief.

I left school in my sixteenth year and went to work first in a builders' office, then for an electricity corporation. I also played piano in a four-piece band for dances all over North Cornwall. My father, victim of World War I, had died in 1924, and the first poets to make a real impact on my mind and imagination were those of that war: Sassoon, Owen, Graves, Thomas and the rest. At the same time, thirties poets like Auden, Spender, MacNeice and Day Lewis, as well as prose writers like George Orwell and Arthur Koestler, helped me (much more than newspapers) to understand something of what was happening in the Europe of my own day. Later on I discovered, particularly, the poems of Hardy, Yeats and John Betjeman.

The year 1940 saw me in the Royal Navy when, among much else, I literally travelled the world, both outside and inside my skin. It's difficult to sit down and write plays or novels at a table on a naval messdeck. But I found that I could write poems in my head when I was working on routine jobs that didn't require much thought. After the war I worked for many years as a schoolteacher in Cornwall, before resigning my job to become a full-time writer.

I write a poem very slowly and think myself lucky if I'm able to get it as right as I possibly can over a period of from two to four weeks, sometimes longer. I never talk to others about what I'm writing: I think some valuable essence and energy might escape in the excitement of the telling. Anyhow, poetry-writing is a secret activity.

I try to write out of my own experience and feeling, and believe that almost all poetry is autobiographical. If I'm fortunate enough to have an idea for a poem, it's always unexpected, like being suddenly knocked over by a bus. I don't think a poet needs to go in search of a subject like some anxious lepidopterist with a butterfly net. The 'idea' for a poem is always a bit vague; not completely formed. The writing of the poem is a kind of disentangling process to try and discover what the idea is really about. The next problem is to decide the form the poem might take: whether as a short lyric, a longer rhyming poem, a poem in free verse, or whatever. If a poem doesn't begin to reveal itself in one form, I try another.

As I have lived almost all my life in the Cornish countryside, the passage of the seasons, old country sayings associated with them, and the way they are linked with ancient religious festivals, have always been specially significant to me. Candlemas, the Feast of Lights, when churches were lit by thousands of candles, commemorates the time when the Infant Christ, 'the light of the world', was first presented by the Virgin Mary in the Temple.

Blood sports of any kind are anathema to me. Something of this, I think, comes into the 'Jolly Hunter' poem, which also tries to say something perfectly serious in perhaps what appears an unserious way. 'Lulu' is a kind of detective story which, as with most poems, doesn't really aim to end with the last line but which leaves the readers, at whatever level the poem might have been read and received, to provide a personal answer. The 'Dancing Bear' story is a true one and was told to me by my mother when she was in her eighties as though it had happened that very morning.

My Mother Saw a Dancing Bear

My mother saw a dancing bear
By the schoolyard, a day in June.
The keeper stood with chain and bar
And whistle-pipe, and played a tune.

And bruin lifted up its head
And lifted up its dusty feet,
And all the children laughed to see
It caper in the summer heat.

They watched as for the Queen it died.
They watched it march. They watched it halt.
They heard the keeper as he cried,
'Now, roly-poly!' 'Somersault!'

And then, my mother said, there came
The keeper with a begging-cup,
The bear with burning coat of fur,
Shaming the laughter to a stop.

They paid a penny for the dance,
But what they saw was not the show;
Only, in bruin's aching eyes,
Far-distant forests, and the snow.

At Candlemas

'If Candlemas be fine and clear
There'll be two winters in that year';

But all the day the drumming sun
Brazened it out that spring had come,

And the tall elder on the scene
Unfolded the first leaves of green.

But when another morning came
With frost, as Candlemas with flame,

The sky was steel, there was no sun,
The elder leaves were dead and gone.

Out of a cold and crusted eye
The stiff pond stared up at the sky,

And on the scarcely-breathing earth
A killing wind fell from the north;

But still within the elder tree
The strong sap rose, though none could see.

What Has Happened to Lulu?

What has happened to Lulu, mother?
What has happened to Lu?
There's nothing in her bed but an old rag-doll
And by its side a shoe.

Why is her window wide, mother,
The curtain flapping free,
And only a circle on the dusty shelf
Where her money-box used to be?

Why do you turn your head, mother,
And why do the tear-drops fall?
And why do you crumple that note on the fire
And say it is nothing at all?

I woke to voices late last night,
I heard an engine roar.
Why do you tell me the things I heard
Were a dream and nothing more?

I heard somebody cry, mother,
In anger or in pain,
But now I ask you why, mother,
You say it was a gust of rain.

Why do you wander about as though
You don't know what to do?
What has happened to Lulu, mother?
What has happened to Lu?

I Saw a Jolly Hunter

I saw a jolly hunter
With a jolly gun
Walking in the country
In the jolly sun.

In the jolly meadow
Sat a jolly hare.
Saw the jolly hunter.
Took jolly care.

Hunter jolly eager —
Sight of jolly prey.
Forgot gun pointing
Wrong jolly way.

Jolly hunter jolly head
Over heels gone.
Jolly old safety-catch
Not jolly on.

Bang went the jolly gun.
Hunter jolly dead.
Jolly hare got clean away.
Jolly good, I said.

My Mother Saw a Dancing Bear

People differ in their opinions about whether animals should be kept in captivity. Large zoos have often been considered to play a useful role in education, and in helping to preserve some species from extinction. But although there are many safeguards, and conditions are subject to inspection, people still object to some zoos, dolphinaria and other money-making 'attractions'. There is no doubt that circuses, although traditionally regarded as places for entertaining outings, upset many people who do not enjoy seeing animals compelled to perform for the amusement of humans.

We do not see 'dancing bears' touring round towns and villages these days, but they were a common sight within the memory of many older people. There can be something very distressing about seeing a wild, free spirit caged or chained, away from its natural habitat. Does it seem even worse, as Charles Causley implies, when man is making money from another creature's misfortune? You could discuss this opinion. And you could try writing about an animal you have seen in captivity. What feelings does it have? What feelings do *you* have? Your teacher could perhaps read you another poem on this subject: 'Jaguar', by Ted Hughes.

At Candlemas

This poem combines a clever, unobtrusive use of rhyme with close observation of the natural world: the 'cold and crusted eye' of the 'stiff pond', and 'the sky was steel'. To say 'the sky was steel' is to use metaphor (see 'Cleaning Ladies' by Kit Wright, page 55). The sky is not really steel, but looks as if it might be, in colour and density.

'At Candlemas' takes as its starting-point a superstition in the form of a country saying (or 'wise saw' as they are sometimes called). We all know many superstitions, some of them even in rhyme. Take a superstition and see if it provides an idea for a poem (a black cat crossing your path, a broken mirror). You can write the poem in any form you wish; but you might try doing what Charles Causley does here. Your rhymes, if you use them, must fit what you want to say exactly. Never let the rhyme decide for you. If you decide to write about a landscape, or a particular scene, make sure you describe it in some detail. Detail always helps the reader to picture the scene more vividly.

What Has Happened to Lulu?

The poet says this is a kind of detective poem in which you, the reader, have to decide what *has* happened to Lulu. There is a trail of clues, but they are open to different interpretations. What do *you* think happened? You might like to compare this with the Beatles' song, 'She's Leaving Home'. Are there similarities?

One technique used here is that of asking questions. 'What?' and 'Why?' are repeated throughout the poem, helping to increase the atmosphere of mystery and give the poem a kind of framework. This is a method which you might like to try, basing a poem of your own on a whole series of questions.

Be careful not to over-use this, or any other idea, but move on to different forms and techniques. The more variety there is in your poems the less bored will your readers be — and you as well!

I Saw a Jolly Hunter

This well-known poem is an excellent example of several techniques, though it is not the kind of poem which can easily be used as a model for your own writing. It treats a serious subject, blood sports, in a truly comic fashion, leaving you in no doubt as to the opinion of the poet. It achieves this by very cleverly doing something which you should generally avoid in writing poetry: using a single word again and again. Charles Causley's skill and humour enable him to use that one word 'jolly' several times over, with slightly different meanings suggested, and make a point by its very repetition. It might look easy, but it isn't.

Stanley Cook

I was born and grew up in Austerfield, a South Yorkshire village with a population of about 500, almost all of whom I knew by name, and have spent most of my grown-up life in Sheffield, a South Yorkshire city with a population of 500,000. Life with a single village shop and buses to town on market day only was simpler and, where a frost at apple blossom time really meant fewer apples to eat later, more direct. Life in the country is the ruler by which you can measure life in the city. If you are learning, it is best to start with straightforward examples and I learnt about people from the straightforward country people among whom I grew up.

My father's father was a blacksmith and my father was an engineer's patternmaker, that is, he made patterns in wood for the real thing that would eventually be cast in steel. If you wonder how he found this kind of work in a small village, the answer is that he would cycle as much as twenty miles to work. I went to Doncaster Grammar School on a scholarship and to Oxford on another scholarship: I like to think that the poetry I write, however much my education was extended beyond the average, can be understood and enjoyed by those whose education was not thus extended. Poets should, in my opinion, write poems that as many people as possible can appreciate.

Since most people still live in big industrial cities or towns, you have to keep in mind, if you are trying to give pleasure to as many people as possible, the kind of thing they can see there. One thing they see, alas, is plenty of litter. But this has a life of its own, rushing down the road before the wind like football fans on to the pitch. In 'The

Performing Bag' I described a moment when a gust of wind in a school playground made a plastic bag take off like a prisoner escaping by helicopter.

The amusements in parks and fun-fairs seem to me all devices to give us for a time an extra power. On a slide, if you can't have the sea, at least you can have the movement of a wave.

Making a poem meant that the significance of the kind of thing I had often seen before at last dawned on me.

The Slide

Like the seagull I saw
Last summer at the seaside
Sitting on top of a wave
That washed it ashore,
On the playground slide
I come sweeping down;
And as for a moment I stand
At the bottom on dry land
Other children follow
Like more white waves
That break on the yellow sand.

The Performing Bag

The plastic bag that once was full
Of coloured sweets was empty and lost
And lay against the playground wall,
Flat and still among the dust.

But a wind came up the road,
Brushing back the hair of the grass,
Trying to unbutton people's coats
And teasing the leaves as it passed.

It felt its way inside the bag
Like a hand inside a glove
And like a puppet waking up
The plastic bag began to move.

As the air inside it puffed it out,
The bag that was lying sad and flat
Began to waggle its corners about
And nodded its head this way and that.

It dodged its way between the children
Who watched it carried high in the sky
And disappear on the hand of the wind
Waving them goodbye.

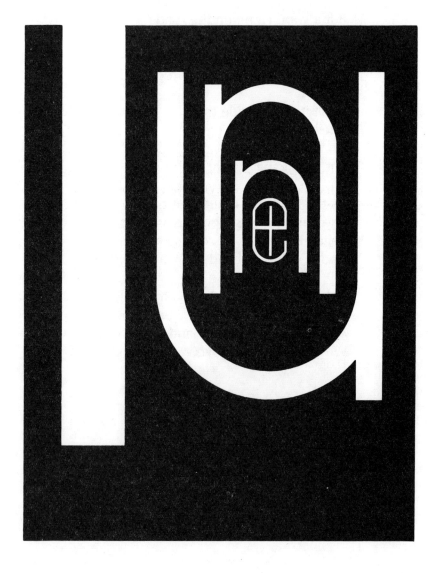

The Slide

The poem begins with a simile: the seagull gliding into shore on the crest of a wave is likened to the child on the playground slide. The feeling of movement — the swoop, dip and slight rise again to be cast upon the ground — is thus made more vivid to us by the use of another 'picture' in which a similar movement is occurring. The sea comparison continues with the description of other children on the slide as resembling a series of waves breaking on to the shore.

Write a short poem about a small incident where you can discover a direct comparison of this kind with something else. Using your chosen simile (saying something is *like* something else), try to extend it throughout the poem, as in 'The Slide'.

The Performing Bag

Here the poet takes a very small incident most of us would not even notice. Although the bag is the performer, the wind is the director and prime mover of the action. The scene is set in the first verse and then the wind enters — almost a person, capable of unbuttoning coats and teasing. Notice the use of metaphor in phrases like 'the hair of the grass' and 'the hand of the wind'. When you use a metaphor you are saying, or suggesting, that something *is* something else: the grass *is* hair. This encourages the reader to observe with a sharper eye and see two pictures at the same time.

Stanley Cook uses a mixture of different kinds of rhyme, including full rhyme ('flat' and 'that', 'sky' and 'goodbye') and half-rhyme, where the words have some sounds echoed or rhymed but not all sounds ('lost' and 'dust'). There is also an example of what is known as spelling rhyme: 'glove' and 'move'. These words *look* as if they rhyme from their spelling, but when they are spoken, the sounds are not the same. You will probably find it easier if you do not try to mix different kinds of rhyme in one poem.

Tunnel

This is a one-word concrete poem. Only the letters of the word have been used, and these have been arranged in a visual pattern to show what the word means. Try taking one word and arranging the letters on the page in a design which indicates its meaning. You can use each letter more than once if you wish, but make sure the word is still visually understandable.

Ivor Cutler

I did not start writing poetry seriously till I was 43, then it took seven years to produce work of professional quality.

The madness with words started when I was 12. I invented a new language with non-English letters. Proudly, I showed it to my Hebrew teacher. He was a bachelor and a failure. 'What can you do with it?' he asked.

Although I enjoyed Latin for its structure, Greek, with its lovely alphabet, fed my love of the strange and different.

At 15, I composed and wrote down in staff notation my first piece — 'Funeral Bells'.

I discovered section 827–humour, and 817–humor, in Langside public library.

At 17, the guitar and folksong — Gaelic, Spanish, Russian, Asian.

At 21, drawing, painting and sculpture.

They were all searches for simplicity.

At 34, I read *The Trial* by Franz Kafka. It matured my sense of humour. Humour suits my melancholy Glasgow-Jewish disposition.

I studied African drum rhythms and play jazz by ear.

I do not know what is inside my head, but I want to communicate it. At 4.00 a.m. I wake up and seize pen and paper. Then I wait. A couple of words surface. I write them down, then slowly, delicately, pull the rest of the poem out. I do not censor the meaning. But I do censor the noise that the words make. Subtle rhythms, flavours, textures. I am influenced too by the nib — soft, hard, thin, thick; and by the paper — size, texture, colour, quality.

In the morning, I look at what I have written and am usually pleased and amused — sometimes thrilled.

So my poem is a messenger carrying a message from my unconscious mind to yours. I do not know how it works, but it does.

I seldom change a word.

I am a medium. Experiences pass through my senses, are mixed and shaped, and exit via the tip of my pen. I just let it happen. I was held of little account at home or school, nor was I popular. I began to respect myself when I was 43. No one, including myself, could have prognosed what I have become.

My sock
is
round my foot.
My sock
is
in my shoe.

How can it
not only be
in two places
but 2 shapes?

Socks
are more cunning
than
they let on.

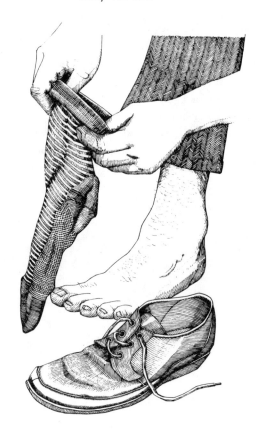

I like sitting.
The best
thing about sitting
is
sitting down.
When you are young
they say,
'sit up!'
That is
stupid.
You can not
sit up unless
your spine is
funny.
I sat up, and
bent.

They forget
they were
young.

My Sock

This is a poem that looks at a very ordinary, everyday object from different angles. Ivor Cutler proves that a sock can be both 'in' something and 'round' something else at the same time.

The words 'in' and 'round' are prepositions, words which change the angle from which you see things. 'Above', 'below', 'through', 'under', 'on' and 'by' are other examples. You might see how many prepositions you know by making a list, but the fun will come in using them. Can you think of any other things that might be said to be in two (or even more) places at the same time?

Choose a subject (perhaps The Sea, The House) and write a series of lines about it, starting each one with a different preposition and describing what you see from its angle (Inside the House, Around the House, Under the House, and so on).

I Like Sitting

Here is another example of a poet's sheer enjoyment of the oddity of language: the expression 'sit down' coupled with the expression 'sit up'. They contradict each other. How *can* you sit up and down simultaneously? What other expressions do this?

Some expressions can seem extremely odd if you think of them literally: 'Wipe that smile off your face!' 'You'll just have to face the music!' 'I've got eyes in the back of my head!' These, and many more, could easily be the starting-point of a poem. Think of a saying and let your imagination build up a picture. Write down what comes into your head and then shape your ideas into a poem.

Alan Brownjohn

I have lived all my life in London — except for a gap of two years during the Second World War when I was 'evacuated' to Cornwall and lived on a small farm. My schooling, in junior and secondary schools, was in south-east London, and at nineteen I went up to Oxford University where my subject was History.

In the first place I wanted to write novels, or short stories, or plays (I was a playground story-teller among my friends in junior school). But at the age of 13 I began to write poems, in a very private exercise-book, and have never stopped since. Those poems are now lost; but I remember them as a mixture of things: poems about particularly personal feelings, poems about animals and incidents in daily life, and some comic poems. I also recall that they came to me in all shapes and lengths, some using rhyme and others not.

Occasionally I would show one or two of the less personal poems (written at about the ages of 15 or 16) to friends, who might say they reminded them of poems by poets they knew I was interested in: Browning, or T.S. Eliot, or John Betjeman. I had to agree. But I did not let that worry me until I decided that I wanted to make poetry a lifelong activity.

I went up to university in 1950, and quickly met a number of other students who were interested in writing. More of them were writing poetry than anything else, and I am sure that the encouragement — and criticism — I had from young poet friends at that time was extremely important in developing my own writing.

After university I became a teacher, then a lecturer in a college that trained teachers, and eventually a full-time writer. I had three fascinating years when I was elected as a borough councillor, and once stood as a candidate for the House of Commons (without success, but without disaster.) All this time I was publishing poetry, and the first of my books *The Railings*, appeared in 1961. I have always written slowly — twelve poems a year is a good crop for me — and I was quite surprised to find I had two hundred poems to put into my *Collected Poems* in 1983.

One of the poems in that first book became, I think, fairly well-known. It tends to be referred to by its first line, 'We are going to see the rabbit', as it has no title. I believe that it is essential to have pen and paper always available, wherever you may be, so as to write down any sudden, unexpected ideas for poems. Sitting on a train which had stopped during a thick fog in outer London, I could see only rooftops on either side. I imagined a dismal future in which there would be no green countryside left in England, only pollution: no grass, and no animal life, except for one last pathetic rabbit. In seconds I had the idea for a poem, and began to write it in a handy notebook.

The two other animal poems here are in lighter mood, and come from a set of *Brownjohn's Beasts*. Some of these humorous animal poems are in rhyme (like 'Parrot' and 'Chameleon') because rhyme can be used to produce a comic 'snap' at the end of a poem. The chameleon is proud of its ability to change colour and disguise itself against any background. In this it is like people who seem able to alter their nature according to the company they are in. You could see this chameleon as resembling a human being who changes so often that he (or she) doesn't know exactly what to think of himself. Or herself. The 'Parrot', on the other hand, is cunningly waiting to take revenge on real human beings who are always trying to fit him into their own neat pattern.

'In this city' — another poem using its first words as a title — is a short and sad little fantasy about loneliness. (Have *you* ever forgotten that someone was in the room when you went out switching off the light?) It is written on the pattern of an object within an object within. . . The 'Skipping Rhyme' uses a pattern of another sort. It takes the idea of a rhyme to skip to, and spins out a mysterious — deliberately mysterious — tale and rhythm which adds up to: nothing. I wanted to write something which would *lead* people into finding deeper and deeper puzzles in the words.

Chameleon

I can think sharply
and I can change:
my colours cover a considerable range.

I can be some mud by
an estuary,
I can be a patch on the bark of a tree.

I can be green grass
or a little thin stone
 — or if I really want to be left alone,

I can be a shadow . . .
What I am on your
multi-coloured bedspread, I am not quite sure.

Skipping Rhyme

Pain of the leáf, one, twó —́
Word óf the stóne, thrée, four —́
Fóot óf the dárk, pit óf the hánd,
Heárt óf the clóud, fíve, síx, and
Out!
  Skíp.
Nóra she had white eýes,
Máry she had bláck —́
Hélen looked in Gréy Man's Wóod and
Néver cáme
Back!
  Jump.
Nóra dráws a gréen thréad,
Máry spins it blúe —́
But Hélen will not bind it till her
Trúe Love makes it
Trúe!
  Quick!
One, twó, leáf of the páin,
Thrée, fóur, stóne of the wórd,
Fíve, síx, dark of the fóot, hand of the pit,
Clóud of the heárt, and
OUT!

'We are going to see the rabbit. . .'

We are going to see the rabbit,
We are going to see the rabbit.
Which rabbit, people say?
Which rabbit, ask the children?
Which rabbit?
The only rabbit,
The only rabbit in England,
Sitting behind a barbed-wire fence
Under the floodlights, neon lights,
Sodium lights,
Nibbling grass
On the only patch of grass
In England, in England
(Except the grass by the hoardings
Which doesn't count.)
We are going to see the rabbit
And we must be there on time.

First we shall go by escalator,
Then we shall go by underground,
And then we shall go by motorway
And then by helicopterway,
And the last ten yards we shall have to go
On foot.

And now we are going
All the way to see the rabbit,
We are nearly there,
We are longing to see it,
And so is the crowd
Which is here in thousands
With mounted policemen
And big loudspeakers
And bands and banners,
And everyone has come a long way.

But soon we shall see it
Sitting and nibbling
The blades of grass
On the only patch of grass
In — but something has gone wrong!
Why is everyone so angry,
Why is everyone jostling
And slanging and complaining?

The rabbit has gone,
Yes, the rabbit has gone.
He has actually burrowed down into the earth
And made himself a warren, under the earth,
Despite all these people.
And what shall we do?
What *can* we do?

It is all a pity, you must be disappointed,
Go home and do something else for today,
Go home again, go home for today.
For you cannot hear the rabbit, under the earth,
Remarking rather sadly to himself, by himself,
As he rests in his warren, under the earth:
'It won't be long, they are bound to come,
They are bound to come and find me, even here.'

Parrot

Sometimes I sit with both eyes closed,
But all the same, I've heard!
They're saying, 'He won't talk because
He is a *thinking* bird.'

I'm olive-green and sulky, and
The family say, 'Oh yes,
He's silent, but he's *listening*,
He *thinks* more than he *says!*

'He ponders on the things he hears,
Preferring not to chatter.'
 — And this is true, but *why* it's true
Is quite another matter.

I'm working out some shocking things
In order to surprise them,
And when my thoughts are ready I'll
Certainly *not* disguise them!

I'll wait, and see, and choose a time
When everyone is present,
And clear my throat and raise my beak
And give a squawk and start to speak
And go on for about a week
And it will not be pleasant!

'In this city. . .'

In this city, perhaps a street.
In this street, perhaps a house.
In this house, perhaps a room
And in this room a woman sitting,
Sitting in the darkness, sitting and crying
For someone who has just gone through the door
And who has just switched off the light
Forgetting she was there.

Chameleon

Here is a poem about an animal well-known for its ability to camouflage itself according to its environment. Whether it can really change its colour and apparent shape as much as the poem suggests does not really matter. The idea is what is important. You may know of other animals, insects, or fish that can camouflage themselves, and you could write about one of them using simple images, or pictures, to show how their disguises work. You might like also to consider *people* who camouflage their true feelings; like those who cover up shyness by being over-boisterous, cowardice by being bullies, sadness by forced laughter, guilt by assumed wide-eyed innocence ('It couldn't possibly have been me!').

Skipping Rhyme

This is an example of a writer taking a traditional form of rhyme and using it for his own purposes. Although it is usually young children who chant skipping rhymes, what attracts them, and adults too, is the rhythm and the often magical-sounding phrases. They are related to superstitions, and witches' chants and spells. If you examine rhymes which you used to know you will find they often include names, colours, precious metals (gold and silver) and birds which crop up in superstitions (magpies, swans, crows, ravens). And, above all, the rhythm is very strong.

This poem does something else, too, with its mysterious phrases. Compare verse one with the last verse and you will notice how the phrases are reversed: 'Pain of the leaf' becomes 'leaf of the pain', 'heart of the cloud' becomes 'cloud of the heart'. Try writing a poem or rhyme using this technique. It will need a good rhythm, and a section in the middle, between the two reversible verses, which is entirely different.

A good way to begin might be to think of some phrases which can be reversed ('light of the star', 'star of the light'; 'isles of the south', 'south of the isles' — but think of your own!) When you have a small collection, see which ones you can put together, and go on from there.

'We are going to see the rabbit . . .'

This poem arises from concern for what man is doing to his environment, something which we have all become more aware of in recent years. The subject is treated with a light touch, and uses humour — often one of the best ways to make a serious point. In its simple use of language the last section makes its message felt, not only about the subject of the poem but also perhaps about what loneliness can mean, as well as how people feel when they are subjected to constant attention from the media or the general public. The message of this poem might well cause you to consider the far more unthinkable consequences of the nuclear age in which we live.

Parrot

It is always a good exercise to try writing from somebody else's point of view. To put yourself into their position, and imagine what he or she would think and feel, requires you to try to know them well in your own mind. Many people find this helpful for their writing (besides, writing directly about yourself can sometimes be difficult). Choose an animal about which you know something, and try writing a poem as if the animal itself were actually speaking: You do not need to use rhyme. 'Parrot' *does* rhyme, but this is a deliberate use of rhyme to assist the humorous effect. Unless rhyme really helps your poem, you will probably find it easier not to use it at first. It isn't essential.

'In this city. . .'

This is another poem which employs a well-tried traditional pattern. You may know an old rhyme called 'The Key of the Kingdom'; but if not, at one time or another you possibly did what many of us have done: wrote your address as Fred Bloggs, 69 The Avenue, Habitown, Castleshire, England, The United Kingdom, The Northern Hemisphere, The World, The Solar System, The Universe.

'In this city' is similar to the idea of a picture inside a picture inside another picture. . . You might like to compare it to a slow zoom-in with a camera, where the shot opens on a wide, overall picture which slowly narrows down to a small detail you could not see at first. Try writing a poem which uses this technique. You might picture a landscape with a general description, and then, line by line, close in on one small detail of it, describing each stage on the way. See if you can give it a *mysterious* effect.

Libby Houston

When I was a child, my nan recited me long stirring narrative poems ('Bishop Hatto' was a good one) she knew by heart from her childhood; and my mother read us poems, too — old Scottish ballads full of murders and magic, *The Rime of the Ancient Mariner*. . . My primary school headmaster was a poet and had us all writing; which was where I began — and never stopped (though really I wanted to be an explorer). Then in the first year at secondary school our only homework was learning a poem each week to recite in class. I was fascinated by the *sounds* of the words, whether or not I understood them. I've always loved listening to stories, and I like telling them in my own poems. But whether I'm listening, reading or writing, I think it is the music in poetry I love most of all — how heard words act together, sometimes fighting, sometimes running hand in hand; how speech rhythms can fairly dance; how you really can *play* words, like music, as well as playing *with* words, to rhyme and pun. . . Anyway, I've been reading my poems out loud now for over twenty years.

But poetry's mostly a solitary business. I was delighted when one day a BBC Schools programme producer asked me to write 'eight poems about insect metamorphosis (and tadpoles)' for radio. 'Black Dot' grew from playing with words until I suddenly found that a few rhymes could tell the tadpole's whole tale. As for the bluebottle fly, I had just broken some good china trying to swat one — which of course got away — so writing its autobiography I felt a rollicking manner entirely suited its exasperating cheek.

'Centrifugalized in Finsbury Park' is quite another kind of poem. It's 'true'. I'd trembled past fairground machines like that for years before I dared, at last, when I was about 35, to have a go. Back on earth, I simply wanted to tell someone about it, and since there was nobody around to tell, I wrote the poem instead. But I haven't written a great many poems (I never remember to count them!). For if some word or line feels or sounds slightly 'wrong', it may take years (twelve years is my record) of rewriting, and turning the poem over in my head, before with luck the 'right' words come and I know it's finished.

Black Dot

a black dot
a jelly tot

a water-wriggler
a tail jiggler

a cool kicker
a sitting slicker

a painting puffer
a fly-snuffer

a high-hopper
a belly-flopper

a catalogue
  to make me
    FROG

Rhymes for a Bluebottle

Some mother or other laid a load of white eggs
    In a rotten bit of food,
And that's how I came into the world —
    And it tasted rich and good!

We had no teeth and we had no legs
    But we turned the stuff to soup,
And slopped and wallowed and sucked the dregs
    In our maggoty family group.

We squirmed in our supper, we twirled in our tea,
    Till we could grow no fatter,
Then we all dropped off to sleep — now that was
    The strangest part of the matter,

For we went quite hard, and brown, like pods,
    And when it was time to rise,
Blow me if we hadn't been born again
    With wings, this time, like — flies!

O I'm buzzing and blue and beautiful,
    I'm an ace at picking and stealing!
I've got masses of eyes to see you with,
    And legs to run on your ceiling!

What's in the dustbin smelling so rare?
    I'm zooming in to see,
Then I'm coming to dance on your dinner — look sharp,
    You'll find no flies on me!

Centrifugalized in Finsbury Park

Hey I just had a go on one of them
things! Didn't notice it had a name,
but anyone could see what it was going to do to you —

something like a giant-size round biscuit-tin without a lid
made of wire-netting, and all around the inside,
niches, like for statues, 30 or so, like coffins, only
upright, and open of course with the kind of lattice —
with a padded red heart at head-height.

Paid 25p, got myself a niche, and stood and waited
with a little chain dangling across my hips,
until it was full, the gate shut, the music started
and the thing began to whirl.

It wasn't the stomach, it was what to do with the head:
no good looking down, but if you let your head back
it felt as if it was going to go on going back, or off —
a bit peculiar, shut my eyes to get through that.

And as it whirled, the whole thing turned on end,
more or less vertical — well, I'd seen that right from   .
the park gates and couldn't believe it, which was why —
and opening my eyes again then, just found myself
lying there — lying down face up, lying up face down
over the whole fairground!

And it didn't make you scream like the top of the Big
Wheel, but smile — look up and everyone else is standing
                                                          there,
hanging there, smiling, look down and you might as well be a
                                                          lazy
bird on the wind, though I did forget I could let go,

and the only strange feeling was,
every time you were on the down side hurtling up again,
you left the skin of your face behind for a second.
You know I've never dared try anything quite like that
before, and it was just very nice!

And when it slowed down and sank down, and all of us
were ordinary upright, and unhitched our little chains,
I only staggered a couple of times, disappearing
on ground level into the dark — and nobody was sick.

Black Dot

This is a poem which follows all the stages by which spawn metamorphoses into a frog. But the method used is unusual: the poem is in kennings. Kennings are descriptive phrases stating what something does, or looks like, without using its name. They were commonly used by the Norsemen in their sagas, and in old Germanic writings (some other examples are 'iron-horse' for a train, 'fire-water' for whisky, 'goggle-box' for television). You can try making up your own kennings for other things; for example, 'mouse-catcher' or 'fur-licker' (a cat), 'life-giver', 'warmth-bringer', 'skin-burner' (the sun). Your teacher may be able to read you a poem called 'The Main-Deep', by James Stephens, which also uses this technique; it can be found in *Touchstones 1*, edited by Michael and Peter Benton, published by Hodder and Stoughton.

Rhymes for a Bluebottle

Here is another poem about metamorphosis, but very different. The rhythm makes it more like a song, and the poet manages to make a rather unsavoury subject enjoyable to read about. There is a tone of delight in the voice of the bluebottle: 'O I'm buzzing and blue and beautiful' (notice the alliteration — see 'The Darkest and Dingiest Dungeon' by Colin West, page 8) You will also have noticed the pun at the end: 'You'll find no flies on me!' The English language is rich in possibilities for puns. We have so many words which sound the same but have different meanings. In poetry this can be used to advantage — and sometimes quite seriously. If you can imply more than one meaning with a word or phrase, you are using language skilfully. Shakespeare was a master of this kind of word-play, as of so much else. You may enjoy reading the scenes in *A Midsummer Night's Dream* where Bottom, the weaver, acquires — and loses — his ass's head.

Centrifugalized in Finsbury Park

This description of a fairground experience may remind you of your own rides on similar machines. Notice the poet's exact descriptions of the feel of the experience. Try to write a poem which concentrates on describing exactly the sensation of going through some unfamiliar, strange or exciting experience — you want to suggest the *physical* feelings to the reader.

Kit Wright

I suppose the main reason for my beginning to write poetry was that my father enjoyed writing it and so did my uncle. They were particularly good at humorous verse in tight forms with strong rhythms, clever rhymes, funny characters invented or described, and witty narrative or dialogue. I loved their efforts and they were pleased when I made, with their encouragement, my own small poems about things that happened or more often about people and things I made up. And in every kind of poem I've since written — poems for adults as well as poems for young people — I've continued to enjoy the 'story' element, the tales you can spin and the situations you can create.

What are the other attractions, for me, of writing in verse? Well, one of them is music. A poem exists not only on the page but in the air as well. It's a pattern of sounds, a verbal tune. And I like to try and make it a strong and memorable tune, one that gets inside your head as the best songs do. It can be quiet or it can be loud, soft or harsh according to the kind of feeling you want to evoke. 'Hugger Mugger' has a particularly loud and harsh tune because I wanted to hammer out the distaste the boy feels at being smothered with kisses by his poor old Auntie! In fact when I'm performing the poem, I always sing the beginning and end of it — if you can call it singing: I've not got much of a voice. I don't think the audience enjoys it much, but I do!

Another attraction is images, the pictures you can make in words to bring the world alive in the reader's imagination. 'Cleaning Ladies' came about because I happened to be Hoovering the floor and thinking: what is this thing I'm pushing across the floor *like*? How would I describe it? And I suddenly thought: it's a cow! It sounds a bit like one and it feeds rather like one, only instead of grazing on grass it stuffs itself full of dust. When I'd finished and the cat came back into the room, climbed into a chair and started washing itself, I thought: what's the *cat* like? Like a vacuum cleaner, Hoovering its fur! So I was pleased to be able to make two images, two verbal pictures that related closely to each other, so that the poem comes full circle. I think, incidentally, that if you can describe one thing in terms of another, you bring it much more alive than if you were simply to say: a cow is a large animal that stands in a field and gives milk, etc. And imaginative describing is one of the things that poetry can do.

'Our Hamster's Life' is a bit of fun about the way we live with animals and pets. I often like, in poems for young people, to give what I think might be the animals' point of view. They can't speak for themselves, after all, and putting words in their mouths is a way of letting them get their own back! As many of my poems do, it contains quite a bit of repetition: it's a way of making things as clear as possible and also of creating the 'tune' I mentioned: nearly all songs have choruses, after all.

'Grandad' is a very different poem, grieving the death of someone who's been very close to you. Time heals your hurt but it takes a long time to go away and perhaps it never does completely. The poem tries to make a memorial in words of the person by 'snap-shotting' particular details of what that person looked like, sounded like. You might like to do the same if you've had the experience of such a loss.

Finally, I don't think any poem succeeds at all unless it gives pleasure. I enjoyed writing these poems — I wouldn't write anything if I didn't — and I very much hope you enjoy reading them.

Grandad

*Grandad's dead
And I'm sorry about that.*

He'd a huge black overcoat.
He felt proud in it.
You could have hidden
A football crowd in it.
Far too big —
It was a lousy fit
But Grandad didn't
Mind a bit.
He wore it all winter
With a squashed black hat.

*Now he's dead
And I'm sorry about that.*

He'd got twelve stories.
I'd heard every one of them
Hundreds of times
But that was the fun of them:
You knew what was coming
So you could join in.
He'd got big hands
And brown, grooved skin
And when he laughed
It knocked you flat.

*Now he's dead
And I'm sorry about that.*

Cleaning Ladies

Belly stuffed with dust and fluff,
The Hoover moos and drones,
Grazing down on the carpet pasture:
Cow with electric bones.

Up in the tree of a chair the cat
Switches off its purr,
Stretches, blinks: a neat pink tongue
Vacuum-cleans its fur.

Our Hamster's Life

Our hamster's life:
there's not much
to it,
not much
to it.

He presses his pink nose
to the door of his cage
and decides for the fifty-six
millionth time
that he can't get
through it.

Our hamster's life;
there's not much
to it,
not much
to it.

It's about the most boring
life in the world,
if he only
knew it.
He sleeps and he drinks and he eats.
He eats and he drinks and he sleeps.
He slinks and he dreeps.
He eats.

This process
he repeats.

Our hamster's life:
there's not much
to it,
not much
to it.

You'd think it would drive him bonkers,
going round and round on his wheel.
It's certainly driving me bonkers,

watching him
do it.

But he may be thinking:
"That boy's life,
there's not much
to it,
not much
to it:

watching a hamster go round on a wheel.
It's driving me bonkers if he only knew it,

watching him
watching me
do it."

Hugger Mugger

I'd sooner be
Jumped and thumped and dumped,

I'd sooner be
Slugged and mugged . . . than *hugged* . . .

And clobbered with a slobbering
Kiss by my Auntie Jean:

You know what I mean:

Whenever she comes to stay,
You know you're bound
To get one.
A quick
  short
  peck
  would
  be
  O.K.
But this is a
Whacking great
Smacking great
Wet one!
All whoosh and spit
And crunch and squeeze
And '*Dear* little boy!'
And 'Auntie's missed you!'
And 'Come to Auntie, she
Hasn't *kissed* you!'
Please don't do it, Auntie,
PLEASE!

Or if you've absolutely
Got to,

And nothing on *earth* can persuade you
Not to,

The trick
Is to make it
Quick,

You know what I mean?

For as things are,
I really would far,

Far sooner be
Jumped and thumped and dumped,

I'd sooner be
Slugged and mugged . . . than *hugged* . . .

And clobbered with a slobbering
Kiss by my Auntie

Jean!

Grandad

When someone close to us dies, we may find we do not know how to cope with our emotions. We do not always know how to control our feelings, so we often shy away from exposing them. One way of helping us to come to terms with death is writing about it, something which Kit Wright has done in this poem. It works by using simple language to describe particular memories. The details building up a picture of 'Grandad' are random memories which will suddenly come to mind about someone you loved. There is no attempt to give a romantic impression of the old man. There is a suggestion of a fond acceptance of Grandad's faults — the very things which may even irritate at the time, but which you miss when they are gone. The particular use of rhyme here helps to lighten the tone — something which needs to be done skilfully, otherwise the poem could become too lighthearted for the subject. The poem touches us by not overstating the sadness. It is implied by the memories, and reinforced by the simple refrain: 'Grandad's dead/And I'm sorry about that.'

Cleaning Ladies

This is a poem using metaphor. A metaphor makes a comparison between two things. But instead of saying the Hoover is *like* a cow, or the cat is *like* a vacuum cleaner (using similes), the metaphor says, or implies, that something *is* something else. When using metaphors in your own writing, it is good to use other words which fit in with your comparison. In this poem the Hoover 'moos' and grazes 'on the carpet pasture'. 'Moos', 'grazing' and 'pasture' are all words which help the 'cow' metaphor to make its point.

You can try writing a one-metaphor poem as an exercise in practising this technique. Choose an object, and write down all the words relating to it which come to mind. Look at your list and see if you can observe a connection between your choice of object and something else. Then write a poem.

If, for example, we look at a pair of scissors, we can list ideas like these: 'pointed', 'two sides which rub together', 'cutting edge', 'dagger-like'. Your poem could then begin: 'A quarrel is a pair of scissors', and possibly go on to talk about 'pointed' or 'cutting' remarks, 'rubbing each other up the wrong way', and so on. This would only be an exercise. But through practice in thinking about metaphor and the metaphorical use of language, your mind will be more alert to its possibilities whenever you write.

Our Hamster's Life

This poem takes a humorous look at the life of a pet hamster. The form of the poem echoes the subject-matter. It seems to go round and round as it repeats certain patterns of words — like the hamster going round in his wheel. The mesmerising effect of watching the wheel rotate, and the tricks which this can play on the eyes, is highlighted by the wordplay: 'He slinks and he dreeps.' And, always, he eats. If you have a pet, you might consider writing about it from an unusual angle. What does it think of *you*?

Hugger Mugger

I should think everyone has had an 'Auntie Jean', or perhaps an 'Uncle Bert', who insisted on giving them that unwanted slobbering kiss. This poem sums up the horror of this common experience, and by a very clever use of rhyme gives us a chance to laugh about it. Do you have any relations with habits which annoy or please you?

The title of this poem, 'Hugger Mugger', is a rhyming compound, that is, a word made up of two rhyming words. Other examples are 'helter-skelter', 'namby-pamby'. See if you can make a list of more of these. Looking through a dictionary will enable you to discover ones which you may not have known before — what about 'holus-bolus'? You will also come across some compounds which are similar but do not rhyme: 'zigzag', 'jiggery-pokery', 'dilly-dally'. You may have an idea for a poem or rhyme of your own based on one of these, or on another compound.

John Cotton

I was born in London and used to live there, but for many years now I have lived in the small Hertfordshire town of Berkhamsted. When I left school I went into the Royal Navy which enabled me to travel to America, India, Malaya, the East Indies and on to the China Seas — this gave me a taste for exploration which I will come back to later. After that I read for a degree in English and became a teacher. All the time, however, I had the wish, the urge, the need to write, and began by writing some long novels not very successfully. It was much later that I met others with an interest in writing poetry, and because of a shared encouragement and criticism I found the way of writing that truly satisfied me.

I found poetry another and splendid way of exploring the worlds of thought, feelings, ideas and experience. So each poem is like opening a door and being surprised by what I find there. That, I suppose, is what 'Through that Door' is about. Each door, indeed each day, offers new experiences and openings into the life of the imagination. That faculty is so important if we are to understand who and what we are, and to understand the life of others and get on reasonably with them. If that sounds dauntingly serious, then I must stress the importance of the pleasure that exploring the world of the imagination gives, and the fun of playing games with words so that they will say what we want them to say.

Perhaps the other poem, 'In The Kitchen', illustrates this better. It is an exploration of a small world of sounds, and the paradox that silence is when you hear things. Just as when we wake in the small hours of the night and, thinking the rest of the world is asleep, we lie and listen to the night sounds, some so delicate that they would be lost in the day's bustle. And how fascinating they are. So standing quietly in my kitchen one evening I began to hear its real conversations. Then, as I played imaginative games with the things I overheard, the poem came.

Through that Door

Through that door
Is a garden with a wall,
The red brick crumbling,
The lupins growing tall,
Where the lawn is like a carpet
Spread for you,
And it's all as tranquil
As you never knew.

Through that door
Is the great ocean-sea
Which heaves and rolls
To eternity,
With its islands and promontories
Waiting for you
To explore and discover
In that vastness of blue.

Through that door
Is your secret room
Where the window lets in
The light of the moon,
With its mysteries and magic
Where you can find
Thrills and excitements
Of every kind.

Through that door
Are the mountains and the moors
And the rivers and the forests
Of the great outdoors,
All the plains and the ice-caps
And lakes as blue as sky
For all those creatures
That walk or swim or fly.

Through that door
Is the city of the mind
Where you can imagine
What you'll find.
You can make of that city
What you want it to,
And if you choose to share it,
Then it could come true.

In the Kitchen

In the kitchen
After the aimless
Chatter of the plates,
The murmuring of the gas,
The chuckles of the water pipes
And the sharp exchanges
Of the knives, forks and spoons,
Comes the serious quiet
When the sink slowly clears its throat,
And you can hear the occasional rumble
Of the refrigerator's tummy
As it digests the cold.

Through that Door

This is a poem written to a pattern set by a repeated first line for each verse. 'Through that Door' invites us to go through and see what is on the other side. And what *is* on the other side is entirely up to us to imagine. Each time we open the door a new landscape is presented to — and through — our imaginations. Nothing in life is impossible. . . in our minds. As long as we have the ability to imagine something it can be accomplished. Words are an extension of our thoughts, and a way of communicating our ideas and fantasies to others.

Write a poem in which every verse begins with the same line, and let your imagination run free. You may look through a window, consider what is inside a book, or suggest what is really at the end of the rainbow. It may be you alone looking, or it may be a series of different people. What would they all like to see (or like *not* to see)?

You may be interested to read another poem on this subject, beginning 'Go and open the door', by Miroslav Holub, the Czechoslovak poet (you can find it in *Watchwords Three*, edited by Michael and Peter Benton, published by Hodder and Stoughton).

In the Kitchen

Sounds are the main preoccupation in this poem, and John Cotton has chosen words which in some way echo or reproduce those sounds themselves. The term for this is onomatopoeia. Onomatopoeic words are words which sound like the things they are describing: 'chatter' (and 'clatter', not used here), 'murmur', 'chuckle', 'rumble' are examples. The idea of the sink clearing its throat implies the gurgling sound as the last water drains down the plughole.

Words for animal sounds are onomatopoeic: 'quack', 'miaow', 'grunt'. You will often find that poems about the sea use words with soft sounds, particularly 's' and 'sh' (waves washing on the shore). They help to conjure up sounds of the sea almost without our realising. Make a collection of onomatopoeic words and try to use some of them in a poem. If this does not work at first, remember what onomatopoeia does and see if you can use it as a device at some future time.

Wes Magee

In 1939 the Second World War began . . . and during that year I was born in Greenock, Scotland. My earliest memories are of sirens and the drone of bombers. Hardly the most pleasant start to one's life.

My father's job took us to a number of towns in Scotland and England, and I grew up in Dundee, Halifax, Sheffield and Ilford, Essex. At school I disliked poetry; it seemed to be either gloomy or old-fashioned. I don't think we ever read a poem written by a living poet. At sixteen I left school and worked in London, as a bank clerk.

Three years later I received my Army call-up papers, and soon found myself in a barrack-room in West Germany. Bored, and far from home, I would lie on my iron-framed bed, reading. I worked my way through scores of novels, short stories, plays and poems.

At that time I bought a notebook and started writing descriptions and character sketches. Soon I was writing poems. Today those first efforts lie in a box in the attic.

On leaving the Army I trained to be a teacher, and I continue to enjoy my job working with primary school children. Not surprisingly I have written a number of poems based on my experiences in education. 'Morning Break' simply lists the activities anyone can observe in a school playground at some time or another. I deliberately did away with full stops and commas so that the poem could develop a sense of speed. This, I feel, helps to create the madcap effect of children at play.

In 'the electric household', which is also a list, I limited myself to the names of appliances and power. The last line, 'ohm sweet ohm', is a pun; there should always be a place for humour in poetry. The poem is more effective if read or chanted aloud.

'Up on the Downs' is very different, and perhaps it falls into the poem-song category. The repeated lines in each verse help to build up a chorus effect. Nothing nasty disturbs the view; the reader is an observer watching the different scenes rather like a bird-watcher in a camouflaged hide.

Morning Break

Andrew Flag plays football
Jane swings from the bars
Chucker Peach climbs drainpipes
Spike is seeing stars

Little Paul's a Martian
Anne walks on her toes
Ian Dump fights Kenny
Russell picks his nose

Dopey Di does hop-scotch
Curly drives a train
Maddox-Brown and Thompson
Stuff shoes down the drain

Lisa Thin throws netballs
Mitchell stands and stares
Nuttall from the first year
Shouts and spits and swears

Dick Fish fires his ray gun
Gaz has stamps to swop
Dave and Dan are robbers
Teacher is the cop

Betty Blob pulls faces
Basher falls . . . and dies
Tracey shows her knickers
Loony swallows flies

Faye sits in a puddle
Trev is eating mud
Skinhead has a nose bleed
 — pints and pints of blood

Robbo Lump pings marbles
Murray hands out cake
What a lot of nonsense
During
      Morning
            Break

Up on the Downs

Up on the Downs,
Up on the Downs,
A skylark flutters
And the fox barks shrill,
Brown rabbit scutters
And the hawk hangs still,
Up on the Downs,
Up on the Downs,
With butterflies
jigging
like
costumed clowns.

Here in the Hills,
Here in the Hills,
The long grass flashes
And the sky seems vast,
Rock lizard dashes
And a crow flies past,
Here in the Hills,
Here in the Hills,
With bumble bees
buzzing
like
high-speed
drills.

High on the Heath,
High on the Heath,
The slow-worm slithers
And the trees are few,
Field-mouse dithers
And the speedwell's blue,
High on the Heath,
High on the Heath,
Where grasshoppers
    chirp
        in the
            grass
                beneath.

the electric household

cooker   blanket
  toothbrush   fire
iron   light bulb
  tv   dryer
'fridge   radio
  robot   drill
toaster   speaker
  kettle   grill
slicer   grinder
  meters   fan
slide projector
  deep fry pan
vacuum cleaner
  fuses   shocks
freezer   shaver
  junction box
water heater
  time switch   lamps
knife   recorder
  cables   amps
door chimes   organ
  infra red
guitar   video
  sunlamp bed
heated rollers
  current   watts
train   adaptor
  bulkhead spots
synthesizer
  night light glow
calculator
  stereo
cultivator
  metronome
volts   hair crimper
  ohm sweet ohm

Morning Break

List poems, of which this is one, are a kind which generally achieve their effect by the accumulation of details. 'Morning Break' is really a (rhymed) list of children in a school playground. Each child is shown doing something — but what is being done is only briefly described. This moves the poem along at a good pace. You could think of it as a series of 'caught-in-the-act' snapshots.

Write a list poem of your own, perhaps with a title like 'On the Beach', 'At the Match' or 'The Class Debate'; try to choose interesting names for the people involved. It is not a good idea to use friends' names: you can surely find others which do not have such close associations.

Up on the Downs

Strong on rhythm and rhyme, this poem has the feeling of a song — and one that delights in its subject-matter. It takes three settings in the country on a summer's day (but how do we know that?). There is life and movement here. Verbs play an important part in highlighting the descriptions of the creatures: 'flutters', 'barks', 'scutters', 'hangs' all help with vivid effects of sound and meaning to make the poem really active in mood. Notice the two similes at the ends of verses 1 and 2, the first appealing to the eye, the second to the ear. Try writing some more verses for this poem, with your own locations ('Down on the Beach', 'Out on the Sea', 'Deep in the Wood', 'Inside the Cave'). Follow the same rhythm and rhyme pattern.

the electric household

This is another list poem, but of a different kind. It merely uses the names of various electrical appliances and arranges them into a rhythmic — and rhyming — poem. The poet is simply enjoying the names of objects which are linked by a common idea: electricity.

You can collect names like this by thinking of some other linking idea: the names of wild flowers, of towns and cities, of sportsmen and sportswomen. You are bound to find that some of them rhyme, so you can then begin to set out your poem with these names at the ends of lines. Say your lists out loud so that you can hear whether the rhythm is right in each line.

Anthony Thwaite

When I was born, in 1930, my father was a bank clerk in Chester. But my birthplace was an accident of timing. Like all bank workers in those days, my father was moved on to a new branch every few years; and when I was three we went to Yorkshire (first to Leeds, then to Sheffield), which was where both my parents came from. My father was a keen amateur genealogist, and his researches showed that the Thwaites, the Mallinsons, etc., etc., had lived in North Yorkshire and West Yorkshire for many centuries.

In 1939, when I was nine, the Second World War broke out. In June 1940, France surrendered to Nazi Germany, and most people thought that the next stage of the war would be the invasion of Britain. My aunt (my mother's sister) had married an American and lived near Washington, DC. So it was decided that I would be sent to America, alone, to live with my aunt's family.

Thus I spent the years between 1940 and 1944 in America, going to American schools and (without knowing it) learning to speak as an American. In American schools I found that my good education in England meant that I didn't need to do very much work; but by the time I came home at the age of 14, my laziness — and the fact that the American schools I'd been to didn't teach French, Latin, algebra or geometry — meant that I was very backward. I went to a boarding school near Bath, where the teachers tried to make up for lost time. Until then, I had no interest in poetry whatever. One day, though, the English master read us some translations of Anglo-Saxon riddle poems, and suddenly I knew that I wanted to write poems — to be a poet, in fact. And from that moment, poetry became one of the centres of my life.

In my teens I wrote an enormous number of poems — sometimes eight or ten a week — but it took a long while for me to begin to write poems that were really 'me'. Perhaps the first of them were written after I left school and had to do my compulsory two years in the army. I was sent to Libya in North Africa as a sergeant when I was 20. I loved my stay in Libya, chiefly because my army work wasn't very hard, so I had plenty of time to explore the splendid ruins of ancient Roman colonial cities which lie all along that Mediterranean coast.

When I left the army I taught for a couple of terms at a private preparatory school in North Wales, filling in a few months before going to Oxford University. At Oxford I studied English language and literature, and went on writing poems. Many of my friends were student poets, and we used to show one another what we were writing, and criticise each other's poems — which can include praising as well as attacking. I met the girl (also a student) who became my wife. When we graduated in 1955, we got married almost immediately, and went out to Japan, where I had been appointed as a visiting lecturer in English at Tokyo University for two years.

After 1957, I worked for the BBC, returned to Libya to teach at the university there for two years, and was literary editor of a weekly magazine, the *New Statesman*, for four years. But since 1972 I have been what is called a 'freelance' writer and poet. I don't think the three poems included in this book are typical of what I write, but often the poet himself (or herself) isn't the best judge of what is 'typical'. 'A Haiku Yearbook' is an attempt to use the Japanese form of poem called the haiku (which strictly should be written in three lines of five, seven and five syllables) to make an image or picture of each month of the year. I wrote 'The Kangaroo's Coff' for one of my daughters (then aged about eleven), just as a way of playing with the strange differences between English spelling and English pronunciation. 'Hedgehog' was written when we lived in the London suburb of Richmond and found that a hedgehog used to come regularly to our back door to be fed: it's really about the contrast between human life and animal life. All three poems enjoy using different forms: the unrhymed haiku, the 'ear' rhymes as well as the 'eye' rhymes in 'The Kangaroo's Coff', and the simple four-line verses of 'Hedgehog', in which the rhymes rather uncommonly come in the first and third lines of each verse, rather than in the second and fourth.

A Haiku Yearbook

Snow in January
Looking for ledges
To hide in unmelted.

February evening:
A cold puddle of petrol
Makes its own rainbow.

Wind in March:
No leaves left
For its stiff summons.

April sunlight:
Even the livid bricks
Muted a little.

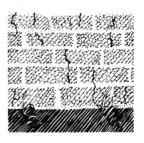

Wasp in May
Storing his venom
For a long summer.

Morning in June:
On the sea's horizon
A white island, alone.

July evening:
Sour reek of beer
Warm by the river.

August morning:
A squirrel leaps and
Only one branch moves.

September chestnuts:
Falling too early,
Split white before birth.

October garden:
At the top of the tree
A thrush stabs an apple.

November morning:
A whiff of cordite
Caught in the leaf mould.

Sun in December:
In his box of straw
The tortoise wakes.

The Kangaroo's Coff

A Poem for Children ill in Bed, Indicating to
them the Oddities of our English Orthography

The eminent Professor Hoff
Kept, as a pet, a Kangaroo
Who, one March day, started a coff
That very soon turned into floo.

Before the flu carried him off
To hospital (still with his coff),
A messenger came panting through
The door, and saw the Kangarough.

The Kangaroo lay wanly there
Within the Prof's best big armchere,
Taking (without the power to chew)
A sip of lemonade or tew.

'O Kangaroo,' the fellow said,
'I'm glad you're not already daid,
For I have here (pray do not scoff)
Some stuff for your infernal coff.

'If you will take these powdered fleas,
And just a tiny lemon squeas
Mixed with a little plain tapwater,
They'll cure you. Or at least they ater.'

Prof Hoff then fixed the medicine,
Putting the fleas and lemon ine
A glass of water, which he brought
The kangaroo as he'd been tought.

The Kangaroo drank down the draught,
Shivered and scowled — then oddly laught
And vaulted out of the armchair
Before the Prof's astonished stair —

Out of the window, in the air
Up to the highest treetop whair
He sat upon the topmost bough
And chortled down, 'Look at me nough!'

The messenger would not receive
Reward for this, but answered, 'Weive
Done our best, and that's reward
Enough, my very learned lard'

(By which he meant Professor Hoff).
As for the Kangaroo, he blew
A kiss down as the man rode off,
A cured and happy Kangarew —

As you may be, when you have read
This tale I wrote lying in bead.

Hedgehog

Twitching the leaves just where the drainpipe clogs
In ivy leaves and mud, a purposeful
Creature about its business. Dogs
Fear his stiff seriousness. He chews away

At beetles, worms, slugs, frogs. Can kill a hen
With one snap of his jaws, can taunt a snake
To death on muscled spines. Old countrymen
Tell tales of hedgehogs sucking a cow dry.

But this one, cramped by houses, fences, walls,
Must have slept here all winter in that heap
Of compost, or have inched by intervals
Through tidy gardens to this ivy bed.

And here, dim-eyed, but ears so sensitive
A voice within the house can make him freeze,
He scuffs the edge of danger: yet can live
Happily in our nights and absences.

A country creature, wary, quiet and shrewd,
He takes the milk we give him, when we're gone.
At night, our slamming voices must seem crude
To one who sits and waits for silences.

A Haiku Yearbook

As Anthony Thwaite has said in his introduction, the haiku is a
Japanese form of poem which is based on a strict count of syllables.
There are three short lines, with five syllables in the first, seven in the
second, and five in the third (seventeen in all). Japanese haiku are
usually about objects or scenes in nature, and are a little like
snapshots. They do not rhyme. A good haiku is like a stone dropped
in water: the poem provides a 'splash', but the ripples are the
thoughts stirred in your mind long afterwards. Each month in this
'Yearbook' is a separate haiku, although you will notice that the haiku
do not all have the correct number of syllables.

Try writing some haiku of your own, on different subjects: you can
tap out the syllables with your fingers. Concentrate on writing three
short lines first; then, if you can make them of five, seven and five
syllables, so much the better. Do not try to say too much; you haven't
the space. When you have written some, why not try a longer poem
where each verse is a haiku? Possible titles are 'A Haiku Clock',
'Haiku Seasons', 'The Haiku Ages of Man', 'A Haiku Week'.

The Kangaroo's Coff

No wonder it can be difficult for people to learn to spell!
This poem shows how hard it is to make rules for English spelling:
there are so many different ways of pronouncing words which contain
the letters 'ough' alone. English is also rich in homophones, words
that sound the same but are spelt differently (hymn and him; cue,
queue and Kew). You might enjoy making a collection of
homophones — see how many you can find.

Hedgehog

If you wrote your own poem about an animal, your use of language
would have to be as precise as possible to be as successful as this one.
Details found in reference books would help you to build up a more
striking and accurate description of the creature. Deciding the length
of lines by rhythm, or the number of syllables, and trying to keep
strictly to a particular form will tighten up your writing and give
shape to a poem.

John Mole

I was born in 1941, in Somerset, and lived in the West Country until I went to university at the beginning of the Swinging Sixties. Swinging has a special meaning for me because, although I have always enjoyed reading and writing, my youthful ambition was to be a jazz musician. I wanted to front a band, and have a powerful rhythm section pounding behind me. I listened, for hours, to musicians like the great pianist Earl Hines. The more daring his improvisations, the more exciting and worthwhile seem the risk involved. 'If you see me smiling,' he used to say, 'you know I'm lost.' I loved the *spaces* between the chords he played as much as the chords themselves. I still love all that and, as a part-time clarinettist, I play whenever and wherever I can, but as the poet I seem to have become, my concern is with rhythms and patterns of a different kind. It's all related, though. I know that the spaces between my words — all those pauses, all that slowing-down and speeding-up — are as important as the words themselves.

As well as being a poet I have found myself a school-teacher and a printer. About ten years ago I joined with a friend of mine (the poet Peter Scupham) in setting up a small press for the publication of poetry. Over the years we have occasionally published a few of our own poems as gifts for our regular subscribers, usually at Christmas, and 'Musical Chairs' was written as one of these. As you can see, it's about a family whose members bring their different rhythms to the occasion, but the poem itself keeps time exactly — tick-tocking like a metronome through a short sequence of rhyming couplets. I enjoyed observing the characters as musical values (*noting* them, in fact) and realising, as I wrote, how the names given to notes are also expressive of behaviour. People can be *crotchety*, or their voices can *quaver*. Demi-

semis sound as if they've got the fidgets. And cats, of course, are also absorbed in their own special music.

My wife, Mary, is an artist, and recently she has been working on a group of etchings of old toys. Some of these toys (which she has come across in museums) are very strange — a squirrel on wheels, a melancholy but exceedingly polite gentleman who raises his hat when you pull a string which dangles from his back. Others are more familiar, like the old favourite who also brought my poem 'Nowhere Bear' into being. In fact, he's reckoned to be the Oldest Bear Known, and you'll see that in Mary's picture he looks it! He's knocked — or *been* knocked — around a bit. 'But,' he says, 'I'm still here.' And that's what the poem is about — still being here in spite of everything, and hoping (at least) for some companionship.

Like 'Musical Chairs', my poem 'Taking the Plunge' was also written as a gift, this time for a class I was asked to visit on the 'Writers in Schools' project. The teacher had sent me some of the class's work in advance of my arrival, and I particularly liked the piece which has been printed here in this book. It had begun as an exercise in the use of speech marks. How *boring*, you may say, but it caught my fancy. 'Flipping 'eck' set me thinking of all the amazed, unbelieving exclamations I could think of. In Hertfordshire, where I live, 'itchy beard' is a playground way of saying 'Oh YEAH!?' The title of the poem is a pun. At the beginning of a relationship you are 'taking the plunge'. And when you begin writing a poem you are doing much the same thing. The fun lies in finding out where it takes you.

As for the fourth poem, it comes from a book of riddles in words and pictures which I put together with Mary in 1979. The book was called *Once There Were Dragons*. In each of the riddle-poems an object speaks in images with which you might associate it, and it asks to be given its name. I based the idea on the Anglo-Saxon riddles, and you can read these for yourselves in the *Exeter Book Riddles*, translated by Kevin Crossley-Holland and published by Penguin Books. I like to think that mine are continuing an ancient tradition. Indeed, as I look back on these notes I've written, I see that I've said quite a lot about gifts and naming, so I'll end by risking a definition of poetry and suggest that it's the art of giving your own world the special name it has been waiting for since the moment you entered it. Or it entered you.

Musical Chairs

Father, weighty as a minim —
Ample the armchair that has him in.

Grandma, like a semibreve,
Rests on the couch she cannot leave.

Mother, an anxious dotted crotchet
Out of the game, prefers to watch it.

Grandpa, a somewhat tiresome quaver,
Is hardly on his best behaviour.

Round him the children, demi-semis,
Fidget and tumble as they please.

The cat meanwhile lies fast asleep,
Oblivious of the times they keep.

Nowhere Bear

I'm a nowhere bear, a threadbare bear,
A ruined bruin, Monsieur Misère
With a moth-eaten coat, a buttony stare
And a bleat of a growl that's beyond repair . . .
Oh it isn't fair, it isn't fair,
I have my pride and I do still care
That I seem rather less than debonair,
So my only hope is I'll find somewhere
Before I surrender at last to despair
An old acquaintance, some kind confrère
From the days when we both had a lot more hair,
Who will take me up in his arms and declare —
You're a still very cuddly nowhere bear.

Taking the Plunge

One day a boy said to a girl in a swimming pool
'I'm going to dive in, are you?' She replied
'No thanks. I bet you can't anyway.' So the boy
got on the diving board and dived and said
'See.' The girl replied 'Flippin 'eck!'
    (Simon Wilkinson/Margaret Wix Junior School)

Flippin 'eck, cor blimey, strewth,
You're my hero, that's the honest truth.

Lummy, crikey, lordy lord,
It's a long way down from that diving board.

Itchy beard and stone the crows,
Don't you get chlorine up your nose?

Luv a duck and strike me pink,
You're slicker than the soap in the kitchen sink.

Knock me down with a sparrow's feather,
How about us going out together?

Groovy, t'riffic, brill and smashing,
Me 'n' you, we could start things splashing.

Watcha cocky, tara, see ya,
Meet me for a coke in the cafeteria.

Hallelujah and Amen,
If you like this poem you can read it again.

Riddle

The Romans built me straight,
They knew where they were going.
I am the quickest route there is
Unless the flies are crowing.

They say, when I lead to hell,
That I'm paved with good intentions.
I have known four strong legs give way
To fast four-wheeled inventions.

I'm what your cheery friend
Says 'Come on, let's have one' for;
And, I'm afraid, if your luck's running out,
When you reach my end you're done for.

Musical Chairs

This could be called a 'pattern' poem. There are a number of different patterns in it, interweaving along a path which to some extent is already mapped out; so, in a sense, the poem writes itself. There is the family — Grandpa, Grandma, Father, Mother, the children and the cat — and each member receives two lines. Then there are the musical notes — semibreve, minim, crotchet, quaver and demi-semi-quavers — each one likened to a member of the family according, partly, to shape but more according to what kind of musical sound they might create. (Semibreves are long notes which slow the music down, demi-semi-quavers are short and fast.) The poem is written in rhyming couplets, that is, rhymed pairs of lines. The cat, of course, just sleeps through it all, not even noticing the 'family music'!

Finding a pattern, or series, to write about can help in writing a poem. It removes some of the problems since you already know roughly what is going on in each verse. Perhaps you could write about your own family, comparing it to a series of some kind. For example, if you take the colours of the rainbow (red, orange, yellow, green, blue, indigo and violet) what colour would your father, or mother, or you be? Or you might try using the days of the week, the instruments of the orchestra, or the seasons of the year. If you decide to use rhyme, make sure you do not end up writing something ridiculous because you cannot think of a good rhyme.

Nowhere Bear

Most people will recognise the teddy bear who has been in the family for a long time: a well-loved, if battered, creature. This poem is written as if the bear is speaking. Writing in the 'persona' of somebody (or something) else is a good exercise. You need to put yourself in the other person's shoes, and try to see things through his or her eyes. This can often allow you to say what you would not say if you were writing as yourself — and to think thoughts which you would not otherwise have had. 'Nowhere Bear' is rhymed throughout according to a particular plan: all the rhymes are on the same sound. This is quite a feat in itself, as it is necessary to choose very carefully the sound you wish to rhyme. Many words have only a few rhymes (and some have none: 'orange', 'sausage', 'secret'). You might like to make some collections of rhyming words and see whether you can use them in a poem. Alternatively, you could try writing in the 'persona' of someone else. Or *something* else. Try hard to *become* the other person or thing, and see matters from this different point of view.

Taking the Plunge

Here is another poem written in rhyming couplets (like 'Musical Chairs' in this section). This time a list of amazed expressions has been arranged to create a poem which is a celebration of an event! Can you think of other expressions (swear-words excluded) which show surprise or annoyance? This expressive, and slightly odd and humorous, use of language does not normally crop up in poems; but we all enjoy using colourful phrases of this kind in everyday life.

Riddle

Riddles have been popular for centuries — the Anglo-Saxons were particularly fond of writing them. Many jokes come out of the riddle tradition ('What's black and white and red (read) all over?' A newspaper.) To write a good riddle you must be able to describe your subject without actually stating its name, and do that in an interesting, well-observed, even witty way. Notice how John Mole has collected facts and expressions connected with roads, and woven them into his riddle. Riddles often rhyme, and this helps them to sound song-like, or magical. Rhyme can be like a cement which holds the poem together — if it is well handled. See if you can write some riddles. Choose your words carefully, and try to make your language exciting and intriguing. Try your riddles on other people to see if they can guess the answers.

Vernon Scannell

I was born in Lincolnshire in 1922 and my very early years were spent in various parts of Northern England and the Midlands with a couple of years in Ireland. My three great passions as a young boy were reading (anything from *The Magnet*, a boys' paper which contained the weekly adventures of Billy Bunter of Greyfriars' School, to the novels of Charles Dickens), swimming and boxing. I discovered the pleasure and excitement of reading poetry when I was about 15 and since then the writing of poems has been my first and most absorbing concern in life. When I was 18 the war against Nazi Germany was declared and I joined the army, serving with the Gordon Highlanders, first in the Western Desert and then in Normandy where I was wounded in both legs. After the war I began writing in earnest, supporting myself by various jobs including spells as a professional boxer, a teacher and journalist before settling down as a full-time author.

The fact that I boxed from the age of 12 to 27 (I was finalist in the British Schoolboys Championships in 1936 and later held a number of senior titles) often arouses a kind of almost disbelieving bewilderment among people who have no interest in, or knowledge of, boxing. This puzzlement is based, I think, on the curious and quite untrue notion that the writing of poetry is an activity practised only by softies. In fact a glance at the history of English poetry shows us at once that many of our greatest poets have been men of action, soldiers, sailors, explorers, statesmen, secret-agents, athletes — just look at the bare facts of the lives of Chaucer, Wyatt, Sidney, Marlowe, Ben Jonson, Sir Walter Raleigh, to mention only a few poets of the past who were not men to trifle with — and the qualities of poise, concentration, self-discipline and quickness of wit required of the poet are not really so dissimilar from those demanded of the boxer. This idea is behind a poem I wrote a long time ago called 'Mastering the Craft'. Now, some twenty odd years after I wrote the piece, I am not sure that its conclusion is true of both fighter and poet; the untrained, crude but strong fighter might be lucky enough to land one mighty clout on a superior opponent. In fact I have seen it happen. But I am now much less sure that the untrained, flabby-minded writer could ever produce a lucky knock-out poem.

My earliest favourites among the first poetry I read were the war poems of Siegfried Sassoon, the lyrics of Walter de la Mare and the sad, haunting and sometimes bitter short-story-poems of Thomas Hardy. Later, of course, I read much more widely and found other writers to love and admire at least as much as those early favourites, but my affection, gratitude and admiration for this trio, and especially for Thomas Hardy, have not diminished. I do not of course presume to compare myself with that great writer when I say that his example may perhaps be seen behind my little narrative poems of ordinary domestic life such as 'Nettles' and 'Intelligence Test', both of which deal with actual incidents involving my own children. 'The

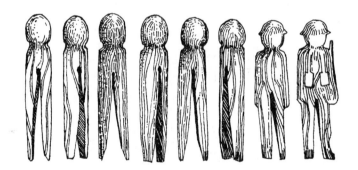

Gift' is partly based on my own infant practice of playing with clothes-pegs and, though the story is fiction, I am fairly sure that it could have happened just as the poem makes it happen. The title is a kind of pun on the word 'gift' meaning the literal birthday-gift of the toy soldiers but, more importantly, that gift of far greater value, the unimprison-able imagination.

The 'Jailbird' poem was written because I know some one (it could be myself) who served a sentence in prison and, after his release, was asked by one of his young children the question: 'What is a Jailbird?' Evidently some of the child's schoolmates had said, not very kindly, 'Your dad's a jailbird!' The convict in the poem is seen as a caged bird. I hope that most of the details are clear enough, though perhaps the line 'Talons long but blunt' should be explained. I was thinking here of the fact that while convicts are given haircuts and weekly baths no provision is made for cutting finger nails. So, unless the nails are bitten, they grow very long like the claws of a bird of prey, but the circumstances of imprisonment render them blunt or useless as talons or weapons.

Mastering the Craft

To make the big time you must learn
The basic moves: left jab and hook,
The fast one-two, right-cross; the block
And counter-punch; the way to turn
Opponents on the ropes; the feint
To head or body; uppercut;
To move inside the swing and set
Your man up for the kill. But don't
Think that this is all; a mere
Beginning only. It is through
Fighting often you will grow
Accomplished in manoeuvres more
Subtle than the text-books know:
How to change your style to meet
The unexpected move that might
Leave you open to the blow
That puts the lights out for the night.

The same with poets: they must train,
Practise metre's footwork, learn
The old iambic left and right,
To change the pace and how to hold
The big punch till the proper time,
Jab away with accurate rhyme;
Adapt the style or be knocked cold.
But first the groundwork must be done.
Those poets who have never learnt
The first moves of the game, they can't
Hope to win.
                    Yet here comes one,
No style at all, untrained and fat,
Who still contrives to knock you flat.

Nettles

My son aged three fell in the nettle bed.
'Bed' seemed a curious name for those green spears,
That regiment of spite behind the shed:
It was no place for rest. With sobs and tears
The boy came seeking comfort and I saw
White blisters beaded on his tender skin.
We soothed him till his pain was not so raw.
At last he offered us a watery grin,
And then I took my billhook, honed the blade
And went outside and slashed in fury with it
Till not a nettle in that fierce parade
Stood upright anymore. And then I lit
A funeral pyre to burn the fallen dead.
But in two weeks the busy sun and rain
Had called up tall recruits behind the shed:
My son would often feel sharp wounds again.

The Gift

When Jonathan was almost six years old
He found a most exciting game to play:
The clothes-pegs that his mother kept to hold
The linen chorus firm on washing day
Were not the kind that snap with little jaws
Like tiny crocodiles; her wooden pegs
Were of the type that gypsies make, and more
Fun to play with. Each had two thin legs
To grip the line, a body, small round head
On narrow shoulders. Jonathan began
To play with one and, when his sister said,
'What's that you've got?' he said, 'A wooden man,
A soldier. Look, I've got a regiment!'
For hours, quite happily, he marched and drilled
His wooden army; then he sternly sent
Them out to fight, to triumph or be killed.
His parents watched his game and, for the day
That he was six, they brought him home a treat —
A box of soldiers, some in German grey,
Some in British khaki, all complete
With weapons and equipment. He'd no need
To use those wooden clothes-pegs any more.
He thanked them for his soldiers and agreed
That they were just the troops to wage a war.
They heard him later, marshalling his men;
The noise came from his bedroom. They crept there
To see the joy their present gave him. When
They peeped inside, the sight that met their stare
Amazed them both; for Jonathan had spread
The clothes-pegs on his carpet for the fray;
The birthday gift was packed beneath his bed,
Neat in its box. The parents stole away.
'Why does he still use those?' the father said.
The mother's smile was one that lights and warms:
'Because they have such splendid uniforms!'

Jailbird

His plumage is dun,
Talons long but blunt.
His appetite is indiscriminate.
He has no mate and sleeps alone
In a high nest built of brick and steel.
He sings at night
A long song, sad and silent.
He cannot fly.

Intelligence Test

'What do you use your eyes for?'
The white-coated man enquired.
'I use my eyes for looking,'
Said Toby, ' — unless I'm tired.'

'I see. And then you close them,'
Observed the white-coated man.
'Well done. A very good answer.
Let's try another one.

'What is your nose designed for?
What use is the thing to you?'
'I use my nose for smelling,'
Said Toby, 'don't you, too?'

'I do indeed,' said the expert,
'That's what the thing is for.
Now I've another question to ask you,
Then there won't be any more.

'What are your ears intended for?
Those things at each side of your head?
Come on — don't be shy — I'm sure you can say.'
'For washing behind,' Toby said.

Mastering the Craft

This poem uses the metaphor of the boxer and his training as a means of describing the training and techniques which a writer requires in order to score points with words. Many people are quite unaware of such techniques, and assume the writer just writes. But there is much more to it than that.

Let us take one of those techniques actually mentioned in the poem: the use of iambics. Iambic rhythm is only one of the very many rhythms available to the poet (Shakespeare was the supreme master of the iambic line, and Vernon Scannell makes frequent use of it). The word 'iambic' comes from a Greek word which means 'limping', and is used because the rhythm is a limping rhythm: de-dum de-dum de-dum. If you say the following line out loud you should hear this rhythm:

The ŏld/ĭamb/ĭc léft/ănd rícht

This poem is written basically in iambic tetrameter, meaning that it has four feet (a 'foot' being a unit of one or more weak syllables and one strong syllable):

dĕ dúm/dĕ dúm/dĕ dúm/dĕ dúm

You can practise writing lines in iambic rhythm. They can have more than, or fewer than, four feet. You will probably find after a while that you cannot get out of the habit!

Nettles

This one tells of a small incident of an everyday kind, and draws some conclusions which should leave us thinking when we have finished reading it. You will notice that 'regiment of spite', 'spears', 'parade', 'the fallen dead' and 'tall recruits' are all examples of military imagery. That is to say, they conjure up images, or pictures, of soldiers — the last line of all makes an impact by that means: 'My son would often feel sharp wounds again.' In this way the use of military terms and ideas prepares the way for the final line and adds texture to the poem.

The Gift

It is well-known that all those expensive presents for birthdays and Christmas are often only played with for a short time. Perhaps they break, or perhaps they are too limiting. Certainly young children are said at times to prefer the box and wrapping paper to the present itself. There may be more scope for the imagination when playing with things that are not so obviously manufactured. Caves or tents made with old sheets and the clothes-horse, boats improvised from kitchen chairs, and so on, can provide hours of imaginative play. Did you ever have games you played when you were younger where you *imagined* you were somewhere and *improvised* what you needed with other objects? This could provide a subject for a poem.

Jailbird

Here we have an extended metaphor (see 'Cleaning Ladies' by Kit Wright, page 55). Taking its idea from the term 'jailbird', the poem describes a prisoner as if he were a bird. Language connected with birds is applied to a man in gaol, and is kept up through to the end of the poem: 'He cannot fly.' Can you think of other expressions which would lend themselves to this treatment? A snake in the grass, a lone wolf, a cold fish, a butterfly? Try writing about someone who is one of these, and use words and ideas associated with the animal to describe the person.

Intelligence Test

This is partly about lack of communication between people, and misunderstanding. Ask a silly question and you get a silly answer. The poem works by building up to the 'punch-line' in such a straightforward way that we are taken by surprise by the 'twist' at the end. Can you remember any time when you innocently, or deliberately, misunderstood a question and gave what you thought might be considered a humorous answer?

George MacBeth

I was born in Scotland in 1932, but my father moved south to work in Yorkshire when I was only four years old, and my childhood was mainly spent in pleasant exile in Sheffield. We would go back to Hamilton, where my relations lived, for Easter and summer holidays, even, sometimes, for an icy Christmas. I still remember Kinburn Lodge, the big old house opposite Hamilton Academicals Football Ground, where my grandmother baked scones and pancake men for us.

There was one eccentric feature of Kinburn Lodge. If you climbed up the dusty stairs to the attic you could stand on tiptoe and get a view of one half of the football pitch through a grimy skylight. Thus I was able to watch fifty per cent of a good number of soccer matches for nothing. Scotsmen enjoy this kind of random bargain.

They also enjoy, I think, a more random kind of poetry than the English do. Perhaps my own taste for strict forms — which ultimately have no logical justification — stems from my Scottish ancestry. It may also be affected — I think it is — by a classical education which had me writing Latin and Greek verse from an early age.

Certainly I do like a poem to have a shape, even if that shape is a fairly casual one. The point, for me, is that some rule of composition — even a very simple one — may help to focus ideas and encourage care in the choice of words.

The poems chosen here are all light-hearted and playful ones. They treat the art of poetry as what, at heart, I sometimes think it may be — a glorious game. It's a bit like the football matches I viewed through my grandmother's attic window, though — a game observed or played under rather original conditions.

'Fourteen Ways of Touching the Peter' is a celebration of a most exceptional cat, my ginger tom Peter, who was unlike any other cat in the world, and thus became known not as Peter, but as *the* Peter — like the Pope, or the Czar, a unique power. Each section of the poem, which tries to capture the fun of playing with a cat — stroking, touching, holding it — is made out of exactly fourteen words. You can count and see if I've made any mistakes, and, if I have, shout 'fault' as at tennis.

'The Orange Poem' is really, I suppose, a poem about writing poetry. It's built on the Chinese box principle of putting one thing — in this case, one idea — inside the other. When you start to unpack them you sometimes think they're going to go on for ever. I imagine there may be a Monty Python element in 'The Orange Poem'. I'd certainly like to see a short film which tried to bring out the weird look of a little man inside a poem eating an orange, etc.

'Old English Sheep-dog' and 'Boxer' are two sections from a longer sequence of poems called *At Cruft's*. You may know Cruft's as the great annual dog show in London, where prizes are given for outstanding canine excellence. I went there once and found myself thinking up a whole series of little poems, like snapshots, which would fix the essence — or at least one aspect — of each dog I liked. Again, as with the poem about my cat Peter, I used numbers to focus my thoughts — in this case thirty-six words for each poem. Poetry, of course, was once called the art of numbers — an indication of how important the element of measure was once considered to be.

'Pavan for an unborn Infanta' is perhaps the oddest-looking of these poems, and you may be forgiven if you shy away from it, at first sight, as something just nonsensical. Well, it isn't, really. Try reading it aloud, emphasising the second half of each word more than the first, as you would in a word like 'belong'. Now imagine that you're a giant panda, doing a mating dance for another giant panda. Right. You've got it.

You see, the words 'An-An' and 'Chi-Chi' are the names of two giant pandas, one of which lived in London and one in Moscow. Repeated attempts — without success — were made to get the animals to mate, but they didn't seem to like each other, and so nothing happened. My poem is a sort of dirge — a pavan, as in Ravel's beautiful piece of music, 'Pavan For a Dead Infanta' — which tries to mourn the little giant panda that never was. Of course, it's a comic, not too serious poem, but I like to think that it has a vein of sadness.

The poet's photograph
of the Peter

Fourteen Ways of Touching the Peter

I
You can push
your thumb
in the
ridge
between his
shoulder-blades
to please him.

II
Starting
at its root,
you can let
his whole
tail
flow
through your hand.

III
Forming
a fist
you can let
him rub
his bone
skull
against it, hard.

IV
When he makes
bread,
you can lift
him
by his under
sides on your
knuckles.

V
In hot
weather
you can itch
the fur
under
his chin. He
likes that.

VI
At night
you can hoist
him
out of his bean-stalk,
sleepily
clutching
paper bags.

VII
Pressing
his head against
your cheek,
you can carry
him
in the dark,
safely.

VIII
In late Autumn
you can find
seeds
adhering
to his fur.
There are
plenty.

IX
You can prise
his jaws
open,
helping
any medicine
he won't
abide, go down.

X
You can touch
his
feet, only
if
he is relaxed.
He
doesn't like it.

XI
You can comb
spare thin
fur
from his coat,
so he won't
get
fur-ball.

XII
You can shake
his rigid
chicken-leg leg,
scouring his
hind-quarters
with his Vim
tongue.

XIII
Dumping
hot fish
on his plate, you can
fend
him off,
pushing
and purring

XIV
You can have
him shrimp
along you,
breathing,
whenever
you want
to compose poems.

Old English Sheep-dog

Eyes
drowned in fur:
an affectionate,

rough, cumulus
cloud, licking
wrists and

panting: far
too hot
in your

'profuse' coat
of old wool. You
bundle yourself

about on
four shaggy
pillars

of Northumberland
lime-stone,
gathering sheep.

Boxer

On a strong
rope,
aggressive,

restrained, you
tug
at your corner,

eager
for the bell, and
to be in,

dancing
round the ring,
belligerent in

your
gloved skin,
muscled

as if to
let fists
emerge, clenched.

Pavan for an Unborn Infanta

AN–AN CHI–CHI
AN–AN CHI–CHI

CHI–CHI AN–AN
CHI–CHI AN–AN

CHI–AN

CHI–AN CHI–AN CHI–AN CHI–AN CHI
AN–CHI AN–CHI AN–CHI AN

CHI–AN CHI–AN CHI–AN CHI–AN CHI
AN–CHI AN–CHI AN–CHI AN

CHI–AN

AN–CHI AN–CHI AN–CHI AN
AN–CHI AN–CHI AN–CHI AN

CHI–CHI

AN–AN CHI–CHI
AN–AN CHI–CHI

CHI–CHI AN–AN
CHI–CHI AN–AN

AN–AN

AN–AN AN–AN AN–AN AN–AN

CHI–CHI CHI–CHI CHI–CHI
CHI–CHI CHI–CHI CHI–CHI

CHI–CHI

AN–AN AN–AN
AN–AN AN–AN

AN–AN AN–AN
AN–AN AN–AN

AN–AN

CHI–CHI CHI–CHI
CHI–CHI CHI–CHI

CHI–CHI CHI–CHI
CHI–CHI CHI–CHI

CHI–CHI

The Orange Poem

Not very long ago
One morning
I sat in my orange room
With my orange pencil
Eating an orange.

This,
I began to write,
Is the orange poem.
I shall become known
As the orange poet

For inventing
And first writing
The original
Perfect
And now famous

ORANGE POEM
Which this is.
Having written which
In my orange room
With my orange pencil

I turned over a new leaf
Which this is.
Meanwhile,
Inside the orange poem
A small man

With an orange pencil
Sat in an orange room
Eating an orange.
This, he began to write,
Is the orange poem.

Fourteen Ways of Touching the Peter

You have probably counted the words in each section already, and found that there are fourteen each time. There are also, of course, fourteen sections. The technique of setting yourself a target of a number of words — your own form in fact — can be a great help in writing a poem. It makes you think just that much harder about the words you use, so that every word has something important to add to your poem. It also gives you a framework, so that you know what you are doing in each verse. Writing about one subject from several different angles is also an interesting and useful exercise. Wallace Stevens did this in a famous poem called 'Thirteen Ways of Looking at a Blackbird' (to be found in his *Collected Poems*, published by Faber and Faber).

Ardent cat-lovers will recognise very easily the different ways The Peter reacts in this poem. You could write about your own pet in this way, or about anything else. You might try 'Thirteen Ways of Looking at' an object, 'Thirteen Ways of Sleeping', or 'Ways of Playing the Fool', or anything else you choose.

Old English Sheep-dog

These are those large, cuddly-looking furry dogs that always seem to be bounding around. In this poem you will notice how George MacBeth has used metaphor (see 'Cleaning Ladies' by Kit Wright, page 55) to describe the legs of the animal: 'four shaggy/pillars/of Northumberland/lime-stone'. This poem is from a sequence of poems, each one of which deals with a different dog.

Boxer

And this is another from the same sequence. The metaphor used here is taken from the dog's name, and the language of boxing has been used to describe the dog (compare this with Vernon Scannell's poem 'Mastering the Craft', page 96).

How many other varieties of dogs can you name (quite a long list)? Perhaps you can write your own poem about a particular breed of dog, and collect together a sequence of poems from other members of your class. It might be a good idea to find a picture of the dog you are writing about, and collect some information which you can use in your poem. Of course, if you know a certain dog personally, so much the better.

Pavan for an Unborn Infanta

As George MacBeth explains, this is almost a piece of music or song for a baby giant panda which never was, because Chi-Chi and An-An did not care for each other and therefore did not mate. Reading a poem like this can be difficult, but if you know the story behind it you might imagine the different stages of the courtship which did not succeed. It could be interesting to try reading this aloud in groups or as a class. Decide in advance what inflexions of the voice you want to use in order to show the action, or lack of it. Perhaps you begin expectant, rather excited at the thought. Then, when the two pandas come face to face, are they wary of each other? Do they then approach, to get to know each other? Why do they not like each other? Do they actually fight? All this can be shown by changing your voice in pitch, tone, volume and expression. There is obvious comic potential here, so you should have fun working up a performance of the poem.

The Orange Poem

As George MacBeth indicates in his introduction, this poem is really a picture within a picture. There is also something circular about it, as it begins all over again at the end — or perhaps it is more a spiralling away from us, a series of the same picture stretching away into infinity. There is a humorous kind of madness here which could also be disturbing — as if you are locked in a repeating pattern (even a nightmare) from which you cannot escape. Trying to write can itself be sometimes rather like that, if you do not seem able to get anywhere near what you were setting out to say! Have you ever had a recurring dream you could write about? Or perhaps you know those Russian dolls which, when taken apart, reveal another, and yet another, exactly the same in each case yet smaller each time? That might be a good subject for a poem.

Glossary

Alliteration: a sequence of words beginning with the same sound (pages 12 and 51).

Concrete poetry: poetry in which the *shape* seen on the page contains the meaning (page 27).

Couplets: pairs of lines, sometimes rhyming (pages 91, 92).

Haiku: a Japanese form of seventeen syllables, divided into three short lines of 5–7–5 (page 83).

Homophones: words that sound the same but are spelt differently (page 83).

Iambic rhythm: a 'limping' rhythm where the heavy stress of the voice falls on the second in a pair of syllables (or 'foot') (page 101).

Kenning: two words linked together to describe something, e.g. fire-water (whisky), ice-box (refrigerator) (page 51).

Metaphor: comparing one thing with another but *not* using words of comparison such as 'like' or 'as'; saying one things *is* something else (pages 20, 27, 60, 101, 102, 113).

Extended metaphor: page 101.

Onomatopoeia: words that imitate the sound of what they are referring to (page 67).

Prepositions: words that change the angle from which you look at something, e.g. on, in, over, under (page 32).

Picture-within-a-picture: where the ideas follow in sequence like 'Chinese boxes' or 'Russian dolls' (pages 42, 43, 114).

Phrase reversal: transposing of words, e.g. 'pain of the leaf', 'leaf of the pain' (page 42).

Repetition: the repeated use of a word, phrase, or refrain for special effect (pages 21, 67).

Rhyme: (full): words that echo exactly the same sound, e.g. 'time' and 'rhyme' (pages 27, 42, 43, 91, 92). (half): words that echo *part* of the same sound, e.g. 'bust' and 'best', 'game' and 'gain' (page 27). (spelling): words that *look* as though they rhyme, e.g. 'glove', 'grove' and 'move' (page 27).

Rhyming compounds: words made up of two parts which rhyme, e.g. 'huggermugger', 'boohoo' (page 61).

Riddles: poems set out in a puzzling way, asking you to guess what they are about from a trail of clues (page 92).

Syllable: the smallest part, or unit, of a word — like one beat in music (e.g. 'word' is one syllable, 'music' is two syllables, 'syllable' is three syllables) (page 83).

Tetrameter: a line of poetry which has four 'feet' (like four bars in music) (page 101).

Vowel-change compounds: words made up of two parts that half-rhyme but change their vowel, e.g. 'dilly-dally', 'zig-zag' (page 61).

Book List

The poets in these pages are the authors of numerous individual books of poetry. Here are the titles of some of them in case you would like to read more of their work. Those marked 'Y' are books written especially for younger readers; the others are principally for older readers.

Colin West: *It's Funny When You Look At It* (Hutchinson) (Y)
Not To Be Taken Seriously (Hutchinson) (Y)
Back to Front and Back Again (Hutchinson) (Y)

Charles Causley: *Collected Poems* (Macmillan)
Figgie Hobbin (Macmillan, hardback; Puffin, paperback) (Y)

Stanley Cook: *Signs of Life* (Harry Chambers/Peterloo Poets)
Come Along Again (Kirklees and Calderdale NATE) (Y)
Word Houses (Kirklees and Calderdale NATE) (Y)

Ivor Cutler: *Private Habits* (Trigram)
A Flat Man (Trigram)
Many Flies Have Feathers (Trigram)

Alan Brownjohn: *Collected Poems* (Secker and Warburg)
Brownjohn's Beasts (Macmillan) (Y)

Libby Houston: *At the Mercy* (Allison and Busby)
Plain Clothes (Allison and Busby)
A Stained-Glass Raree Show (Allison and Busby)

Kit Wright: *Bump-Starting the Hearse* (Hutchinson)
The Bear Looked Over the Mountain (Salamander Imprint)
Hot Dog (Kestrel, hardback; Puffin, paperback) (Y)
Rabbiting On (Armada Lion) (Y)

John Cotton: *Kilroy Was Here* (Chatto and Windus/Hogarth Press)
Old Movies (Chatto and Windus/Hogarth Press)

Wes Magee: *No Man's Land* (Blackstaff Press)
Urban Gorilla (School of English Press, Leeds University)

Anthony Thwaite: *Poems 1953-1983* (Secker and Warburg)

John Mole: *In and Out of the Apple* (Secker and Warburg)
Feeding the Lake (Secker and Warburg)
Once There Were Dragons (Deutsch) (Y)

Vernon Scannell: *Winterlude* (Robson Books)
New and Collected Poems (Robson Books)
Mastering the Craft (Pergamon) (Y)

George MacBeth: *Poems from Oby* (Secker and Warburg)
Poems of Love and Death (Secker and Warburg)
Noah's Journey (Macmillan) (Y)

Writers in Schools Scheme

You may like to take the opportunity of actually meeting poets in person. Many poets are willing to visit schools, and teachers can arrange visits through a scheme administered by the Regional Arts Associations, the addresses of which are printed below.

Regional Arts Associations (England)

Eastern Arts Association
Literature Officer
8/9 Bridge Street
Cambridge
CB2 1UA
(Tel: 0223 357596/7/8)

Bedfordshire, Cambridgeshire, Essex, Hertfordshire, Norfolk and Suffolk

East Midlands Arts Association
Literature Officer
Mountfields House
Forest Road
Loughborough
Leicestershire
LE11 3HU
(Tel: 0509 218292)

Derbyshire (excluding High Peak District), Leicestershire, Northamptonshire, Nottinghamshire, Buckinghamshire

Greater London Arts Association
Literature Officer
25/31 Tavistock Place
London
WC1H 9SF
(Tel: 01 388 2211)

The area of the 32 London Boroughs and the City of London

Lincolnshire and Humberside Arts
Literature Officer
St Hugh's
Newport
Lincoln
LN1 3DN
(Tel: 0522 33555)

Lincolnshire and Humberside

Merseyside Arts
Literature Officer
Bluecoat Chambers
School Lane
Liverpool
L1 3BX
(Tel: 051 709 0671)

Metropolitan County of
Merseyside, District of West
Lancashire, Ellesmere Port and
Halton Districts of
Cheshire

Northern Arts
Literature Officer
10 Osborne Terrace
Newcastle upon Tyne
NE2 1NZ
(Tel: 0632 816334)

Cleveland, Cumbria, Durham,
Northumberland, Metropolitan
Country of Tyne and Wear

North West Area
Literature Officer
12 Harter Street
Manchester
M1 6HY
(Tel: 061 228 3062)

Greater Manchester, High Peak
District of Derbyshire,
Lancashire (except District of
West Lancashire), Cheshire
(except Ellesmere Port and
Halton Districts)

Southern Arts Association
Literature Officer
19 Southgate Street
Winchester
SO23 7EB
(Tel: 0962 55099)

Berkshire, Hampshire, Isle of
Wight, Oxfordshire, West
Sussex, Wiltshire, District of
Bournemouth, Christchurch
and Poole

South East Arts Association
Literature Officer
9/10 Crescent Road
Tunbridge Wells
Kent
TN1 2LU
(Tel: 0892 41666)

Kent, Surrey and East Sussex

South West Arts
Literature Officer
Bradninch Place
Gandy Street
Exeter
Devon
EX4 3LS
(Tel: 0392 218188)

Avon, Cornwall, Devon, Dorset
(except District of
Bournemouth, Christchurch
and Poole), Gloucestershire,
Somerset

West Midlands Arts
Literature Officer
Brunswick Terrace
Stafford
ST16 1BZ
(Tel: 0785 59231)

County of Hereford and
Worcester, Metropolitan
County of West Midlands,
Shropshire, Staffordshire,
Warwickshire

Yorkshire Arts Association
Literature Officer
Glyde House
Glydegate
Bradford
Yorkshire
BD5 0BQ
(Tel: 0274 723051)

North Yorkshire, South
Yorkshire, West Yorkshire

For details of schemes existing in Wales, Scotland and Ireland, write
to the appropriate Arts Councils:

Welsh Arts Council
Holst House
9 Museum Place
Cardiff
CF1 3NX
(Tel: 0222 394711)

Arts Council of Northern Ireland
181A Stranmillis Road
Belfast
BT9 5DU
(Tel: 0232 663591)

Scottish Arts Council
19 Charlotte Square
Edinburgh
EH2 4DF
(Tel: 031 226 6051)

Art Council of Eire
70 Merrion Square
Dublin 2
Republic of Ireland
(Tel: 0001 764685)

Index

Acknowledgments

The publisher and editors would like to thank the following for permission to reproduce copyright material in this book.

Macmillan Publishers Ltd for 'Chameleon' and 'Parrot' from *Brownjohn's Beasts* by Alan Brownjohn, and Martin Secker and Warburg Ltd for 'Skipping Rhyme', 'We are going to see the rabbit' and 'In this city . . .' from *Collected Poems* by Alan Brownjohn; David Higham Associates Ltd on behalf of the author for 'My Mother Saw a Dancing Bear', 'At Candlemas', 'What Has Happened to Lulu?' and 'I Saw a Jolly Hunter' from *Figgie Hobbin* by Charles Causley, published by Macmillan Publishers Ltd; Stanley Cook for his poems 'The Slide' and 'The Performing Bag' from *Come Along Again,* published by Kirklees and Calderdale Branch of the National Association for the Teaching of English, and for his concrete poem 'Tunnel'; John Cotton for his poems 'In the Kitchen' and 'Through that Door'; Ivor Cutler for his poems 'My sock' and 'I like sitting', originally published in *Many Flies have Feathers* (Trigram Press); Libby Houston for her poems 'Black Dot' and 'Rhymes for a Bluebottle', and Allison and Busby Ltd for 'Centrifugalised in Finsbury Park' from *At the Mercy* by Libby Houston; Anthony Sheil Associates on behalf of the poet for 'The Orange Poem' from *The Orlando Poems*, and 'Fourteen Ways of Touching the Peter', 'Old English Sheep-dog', 'Boxer' and 'Pavan for an Unborn Infanta' from *The Night of Stones* by George MacBeth, both books published by Macmillan Publishers Ltd; Wes Magee for his poems 'Morning Break', 'the electric household' and 'Up on the Downs'; John Mole for his poems 'Musical Chairs', 'Taking the Plunge' and 'Riddle', and Martin Secker and Warburg Ltd for 'Nowhere Bear' from 'Penny Toys' from *In and Out of the Apple* by John Mole; Vernon Scannell for his poems 'Mastering the Craft', 'The Gift', 'Jailbird' and 'Nettles', originally published in *Mastering the Craft* (Pergamon Press Ltd), and for 'Intelligence Test', originally published in *The Apple Raid* (Chatto and Windus Ltd); Anthony Thwaite for his poem 'The Kangaroo's Coff', and Martin Secker and Warburg Ltd for 'A Haiku Yearbook' and 'Hedgehog' from *Poems 1953-1983* by Anthony Thwaite; Hutchinson Publishing Group Ltd for 'The Darkest and Dingiest

Dungeon' from *Not to be Taken Seriously* by Colin West, and Colin West for his poem 'A Scarecrow Remembers'; Penguin Books Ltd for 'Cleaning Ladies' and 'Hugger Mugger' from *Hot Dog and Other Poems* by Kit Wright, text copyright © 1981 Kit Wright, and William Collins Sons and Co. Ltd for 'Grandad' and 'Our Hamster's Life' from *Rabbiting On* by Kit Wright.

Thanks are also due to Mary Norman for kindly providing a print of her etching 'The Oldest Bear Known' (page 85), to Joyce Edwards, ATD, for the photograph of Ivor Cutler, to Toby Cotton for the photograph of John Cotton, to Brian Donnan for the photograph of Wes Magee, to Allan Titmuss for the photograph of Anthony Thwaite, Parkers for the photograph of Charles Causley, Lisbeth H Hansen for the photograph of Vernon Scannell, and for other photographs the BBC Hulton Picture Library (page 15), Sally and Richard Greenhill (pages 23 and 35), John Topham Ltd (page 69). The photograph of the 'Round-up' on page 48 is reproduced by kind permission of *The World's Fair* magazine; the drawing of the parrot on page 34 is kindly loaned by Carol Lawson and originally appeared in *Brownjohn's Beasts*; and the line illustrations (pages 30, 45, 53, 63, 78, 79, 94-5, 104) are by Darren Rees.